CONSTRUCTIVE LIVING MIXED REFLECTIONS

David K. Reynolds, Ph.D.

2013

Foreword

For those of you not yet familiar with Constructive Living, CL is a bringing together and extension of two Japanese psychotherapies and their underlying philosophies for daily life. The two original systems are called Morita therapy and Naikan therapy. Both were developed in this century, but their roots extend back for hundreds of years into the history of East Asia. Morita was a professor of psychiatry at Jikei University School of Medicine in Tokyo. Yoshimoto was a successful businessman who retired to become a lay priest in Nara. Morita's method has its origins in Zen Buddhist psychology (not Zen Buddhist religion), and Yoshimoto's Naikan has its origins in Jodo Shinshu Buddhist psychology. Neither of these systems requires that one believe in Buddhism or have faith in anything other than one's own experience. They work as well for Christians and Moslems and Jews as for Buddhists. Both are built on the naturalistic observations of humans and on careful introspection by their founders. I think that as you read about Constructive Living you will be thinking that it isn't so very mystical and Oriental, but rather practical and human and, well, "realistic." The Morita side of CL emphasizes the action aspect of life, and the Naikan side of CL emphasizes the reflection aspect of life.

Action in life

Feelings are an important part of human life. There are feelings we like (feelings like confidence and love and happiness and satisfaction) and feelings we don't like (like loneliness and depression and fear and timidity). It isn't surprising that we try to generate some feelings and eliminate others. The problem with feelings, however, is that we cannot control them directly by our wills. We cannot sit down and concentrate and make our shyness go away or make ourselves stop feeling lonely on a Saturday night or make ourselves fall in love or out of love with someone. It just cannot be done. We cannot make ourselves stop feeling nervous before an exam, or anxious before asking someone out on a date, or tense before a job interview. Feelings are natural consequences of who we are and the situations we are in just like clouds are natural consequences of temperatures and pressures and humidity and so forth. Feelings are natural, and, naturally, they are just as uncontrollable as the weather.

Now, no one tries to fight with rain or fog. You never see anyone going outside waving a sword or a karate blow at rain clouds. And no ordinary humans try by their wills to make fog go away. No one ignores the weather, but we have all learned to dim our headlights in the fog, stay inside during hurricanes, and so forth. And we do what we can reasonably do while waiting for bad weather to pass.

Feelings are just like that. The best way to handle unpleasant feelings is to recognize them (don't try to ignore them or pretend they aren't there), to accept them (you can't control them directly, why try to fight something you can't defeat anyway?), and to go on about doing what you need to do. Rain or fog may not stop you from going to school or to work, but you will take the weather into consideration while driving. In the same way, anxiety need not stop you from studying or asking for a raise in pay, though you'll take it into consideration while selecting a place and time to study or a proper moment to approach your boss. And, in time, unpleasant feelings pass, just like snowstorms. Grief, for example, never sustains its intensity forever. It fades little by little over time unless something comes along to restimulate it again, then it fades again. Just like changeable weather.

As you can see, I'm making a clear distinction between feelings and behavior. Feelings are natural phenomena, uncontrollable directly by our will; they come and go like weather. Behavior (preparing for an interview, for example, or dealing with a difficult client) is controllable. We can choose to dress properly for an interview (behavior) even though we cannot choose to get rid of our anxiety (feeling) about it. We can ask someone out on a date (behavior) while feeling shy. We can total up the check at a restaurant (behavior) even though we cannot choose to avoid our unpleasant feelings about making others wait while we do so. Just as we can decide to go on a picnic even though the day is windy. This distinction between directly controllable behavior and directly uncontrollable feelings is a key feature of Moritist thought.

If we have no direct control over something, we cannot be held responsible for it. Who is responsible for an earthquake? We aren't responsible for having angry, spiteful, depressed, sexy, grumpy, greedy or any other kind of feelings. Again, feelings are natural. On the other hand, we are responsible for what we do, our behavior, no matter what we are feeling. Behavior (except for a few areas like stuttering and sexual impotence and trembling) is controllable by our will, so we are responsible for that aspect of our lives all the time. To be sure, we find it convenient to try to escape from our responsibility for our actions by blaming our feelings. "I was so angry I couldn't help hitting him," "I was too distraught to thank her," "I feel the need for drugs is so strong that I steal to get them." But these feeling-based excuses don't hold water. Similarly, blaming parents or society or spouses or children for our destructive behavior is to seek to avoid responsibility for what is rightfully our own responsibility, no matter what past experiences we may have suffered through.

One of the interesting things about humans is that what we do (our behavior) often influences how we feel. We never have direct control over our natural feelings, but sometimes we can affect our affect by our actions. If you don't feel like going on a job interview one morning it seems to me that it is a waste of time to try to make yourself want to do so. I think it is natural to feel some hesitation about laying your ego on the line for someone else to decide whether you are worthy of hiring or not. There is no need to make yourself enjoy job interviews. The solution? Simply to get out of bed, get dressed for the interview, and go. Sometimes, in the dressing and reading over your resume and driving over to the appointment a sort of excitement and interest in what will happen arises. Sometimes it doesn't. In either case, the interview gets done. Doing a few job interviews well, succeeding at them, having jobs offered to you as a result, may make job hunting even pleasurable. But lying in bed, putting off getting up, and failing to show up for the job interview never gives you a chance to succeed, never gives you a chance to feel anything but uncomfortable about job interviews. The more we allow feelings to govern our lives, the more they spread to govern even larger areas of life.

So we can use our behavior to give ourselves the chance to succeed at accomplishing our goals. And that success often produces confidence and other satisfying feelings.

Pleasant feelings fade over time just as unpleasant ones do, unless something happens to restimulate those feelings. Romantic love fades in a lot of marriages. Respect for individuals and school spirit and patriotic feelings toward one's country can be expected to fade unless restimulated somehow. That's what dates and rallies and national anthems are about. In the doing of these things certain feelings are likely to be stimulated or restimulated. If you want to keep love in your relationship you must keep doing kindness for your partner. As you behave in thoughtful, loving ways you are increasing the chances of sustaining feelings of love for him or her. Romance in a marriage is sustained by gifts and candle-lit dinners and kisses and dressing up for each other and so forth.

But even this focus on influencing feelings indirectly through behavior is a bit unnatural. Sometimes you seem to do everything right, you plan the proper behaviors to generate certain feelings, and the feelings don't turn out as expected. A better strategy for living is to be purpose-focused instead of being feeling-focused. Let the feelings take care of themselves while you go about accomplishing your goals through your behavior. As the emphasis in your life turns more and more toward using controllable behavior to achieve your goals life steadies down and becomes more satisfying. I am not talking here of the tunnel vision workaholic who focuses only on business and economic success. Purposes and goals are various. But, on the whole, being purpose-oriented will pay off more than being feeling-oriented simply because the latter isn't a game you can win with any consistency. You can't make good feelings last and last; you can't make bad feelings go away at will. (Technically, it isn't proper to use words like "good" and "bad" when referring to feelings; like seasons, they have no moral qualities.)

Morita therapy holds that all humans are oversensitive to their own faults and limits to some degree. Especially when we are ill or under stress we may become fixated on some mental/physical disturbance. We blow out of proportion the ringing in our ears or our stiff shoulders or our fear of flying or our discomfort about eating in restaurants or whatever. The proper course to alleviate these problem areas is not to ignore them or to fight them, but to accept them while getting on about proper, constructive behavior. In other words, whatever is troubling us, it is important to accept the troubled feelings and get on about living. Of course, if there is something practical and concrete we can do to alleviate the cause of the problem (such as seeing a physician to rule out organic illness), that is included in the category of proper, constructive behavior.

In general, the stronger we desire something, the more we want to succeed, the greater our anxiety about failure. Our worries and fears are reminders of the strength of our positive desires. They are also reminders of our needs to use caution, prepare materials to avoid the embarrassment of lack of preparation, work hard, practice perfecting our skills, develop our ability to persist and endure, attack the environmental circumstances which caused them, and so forth. Our anxieties are indispensable for us in spite of the discomfort accompanying them. To try to do away with them would be foolish. Morita therapy is not really a psychotherapeutic method for getting rid of "symptoms." It is more an educational method for outgrowing our self-imposed limitations. Through Moritist methods we learn to accept the naturalness of ourselves.

In their advanced stages CL students accept themselves as part of the natural situation in which they are embedded. I do not refer to some passive conformity, but to a dynamic recognition that we exist as situationally-embedded aspects of Reality. We take on our identities from the circumstances in which we find ourselves. We are rather like the cursor markers on the computer screen of Reality. The loss of self- centeredness, in more than one sense of the word, is an ultimate goal for some students of this method. However, relief from the obsessive pressure of phobias, anxieties, and psychosomatic difficulties is sufficient for many students.

Reflection on life

One of the factors that seems to influence how we feel is our attitude toward the world. If we are constantly concerned with getting our share, with making sure we aren't left out, if we are extremely self-focused and self-conscious then we are likely to have a lot of miserable feelings. The world just never seems to send us green lights and lottery prizes and kind words when we want them. And we want them nearly all the time.

Have you ever stopped to think about how much of you is truly yours? Your name was given to you by your parents. So was your body. The words you use were taught to you by parents and peers and teachers. Your body has grown and is sustained by food that people you don't even know produced and processed for you. The clothes you wear were created and sewn by others, bought with money given you by someone else. Even the ideas you have seem to bubble to the surface of your mind, coming out of nowhere and passing along to be replaced by other thoughts from nowhere. There's nothing that is truly yours; it is all borrowed. Of course, it is the same for all of us.

You may say, of course, that you bought your clothes with your own money. But who gave you the money? Who taught you to do the work you do which earned the money? Who hired you? Who gave you the basic educational skills to learn the trade you ply? The point is that when we trace back our achievements far enough we see the fruits of others' efforts in our behalf, inevitably. We have done nothing on our own.

Strange, then, that we should have the notion that we are "self-made." We believe that we got where we are by our own efforts. With just a little bit of reflection we can see that such notions of having come this far on our own are laughable. Deeper reflection allows us to see in even greater detail how we have been and continue to be supported on all sides in all sorts of ways by people and things and energies (such as electricity and the sun's heat and light).

One result of sorting out the specific, concrete ways in which the world supports us (just as you are supporting me now by loaning me your eyes to read this chapter) is a feeling of gratitude. I don't deserve all this help from you and this paper and the electricity that powers this word processor (and the people who worked to generate this electricity), and the editor and publisher of this book, and the manufacturers of this printer's ink, book designers, and the people who taught me these lifeways, and so forth. But, through Naikan, we can come to notice and appreciate the surrounding nurturance from the world and to offer words of thanks. Before I underwent a week of Naikan training in Japan, I thought all this was my due. I took it for granted, and drift back into that attitude sometimes still. But whether I recognize it or not, whether I accept it or not, whether I feel gratitude or not, whether I try to return the favors or not, Reality keeps on being what it is. It keeps on giving to me, not in some abstract sense, but concretely, through Jim and Frank and Lynn and this keyboard and so forth.

So the natural response to realizing what is really going on is the desire to repay and a sort of guilt when we see that we haven't been doing much repaying right along. Starting with our parents our attitude shifts from how little we have received from them and how much more they owe us to one of how much we have received from them and how important it is to start working on giving back something to them. I'm not suggesting that all parents are perfect and that they have done a perfect job in raising us. But I am asserting that there were some adults in our lives who fed and clothed us and nurtured us when we were small. They did it whether they were in the mood or not, over and over again, whether we felt appreciative or showed them gratitude or not--or we wouldn't have survived to be here today.

The gratitude and desire to repay apply to the people in your life today, as well, and to objects in your world. What have you done for your shoes lately, for your car, for electricity, for your toothbrush and stereo set? If you take a moment to consider what they have done for you, it seems not quite so odd to think of what you might do for them in return.

I've never met a suffering neurotic person who was filled with gratitude. Isn't that something? Gratitude and neurotic suffering seem to be antagonistic. If there is anything characteristic of neurosis it is a self-centeredness. Gratitude, on the other hand, is other-centered. It carries with it the desire to serve others in repayment, even if it causes some inconvenience to oneself.

Introduction

I have worked on the development of Constructive Living (CL) for more than forty years after my years of teaching at UCLA and the USC School of Medicine. Adapting ideas from Japanese psychotherapies and Eastern thought CL offers a sensible way of living to Westerners as well as to those in its countries of origin. Adding fresh, modern elements and avoiding mystical Oriental baggage I presented CL in the West through academic channels (University of Hawaii Press, University of California Press, SUNY Press, University of Chicago Press) and popular press books (in the United States, Japan, England, China, Germany, Australia, India, Czechoslovakia, and Mexico), and magazines and newspapers ("O" Magazine, Cosmopolitan, USA Today, New Dimensions, American Health, New Woman, Self, The Japan Times, The Sun, Men's Health, and elsewhere). More than 300 CL instructors have been certified, including citizens of the United States, Japan, Canada, England, Germany, Australia, New Zealand, Mexico, South Africa, the Philippines, and Poland. Across cultures and generations CL ideas make sound, practical sense.

In this book I consider what a CL interpretation has to offer some classic human writings-from Confucianism to Christianity to Buddhism to a secular philosophy. The chapters below are not retranslations in any sense, merely CL reflections stimulated by the classic contributions to literature. This volume follows in the line of my earlier works on Taoism (*Reflections on the Tao te Ching*) and Zen (*Light Waves: Fine Tuning the Mind*).

FOREWORD

INTRODUCTION

CONTENTS

REFLECTIONS ON THE SONG OF CH'AN TAO CHIA—THE TWENTY-SEVEN PRECEPTS OF TAOISM

REFLECTIONS ON THE SAYINGS OF CONFUCIUS

REFLECTIONS ON THE TRACT OF THE QUIET WAY

REFLECTIONS ON THE SONG OF CH'AN TAO CHIA—THE TWENTY-SEVEN PRECEPTS OF TAOISM

Here I list the original translation of each Taoist precept (translated by Stan Rosenthal) followed by a related Constructive Living precept in italics. Thus, you can see the similarities and differences.

Have compassion for all sentient beings causing them no unnecessary hurt nor needless harm.

However you feel about beings and objects cause them no unnecessary hurt or harm by your behavior.

Refrain from needless competitiveness, from contriving for self-advantage and from subjugating others.

You need not compare yourself with others, either aiming for superiority or emphasizing your relative weaknesses.

When accepting authority over others know also that you accept responsibility for their wellbeing.

You are responsible only for what you do, not for anyone else. Nevertheless, what you do may affect others. The results of what you do are not completely under your control.

Value true friendship and fulfill your obligations rather than striving with egotistical motive.

Whatever your motives may be, fulfill your obligations. Find and hold worthy values.

Seek liberation from the negative passions of hatred, envy, greed and rage, and especially from delusion, deceit and sensory desire.

Passions, feelings, are not under your control. Accept whatever emotions appear and act in honorable, righteous ways.

Learn to let go of that which cannot be owned or which is destroyed by grasping.

Don't waste time and energy trying to control the uncontrollable or own that which cannot be owned. Notice what behaviors lead to unnecessary misery and avoid them.

Seek the courage to be; defend yourself and your convictions.

Defend what is right, feeling courageous or not.

Accept transience, the inevitable and the irrevocable.

Accept reality as it is. Then act to change it when necessary.

Know that change exists in everything.

Change happens. We all have "many me's".

Negate the barriers to your awakening. Discover the positive in the negative and seek a meaningful purpose in what you do.

Learn from what reality brings you. Act with meaningful purpose.

Be just and honorable. Take pride in what you do rather than being proud of what you have accomplished.

Do what is right to do. Pride is the uncontrollable feeling that sometimes accompanies accomplishment.

Having humility and respect, give thanks to those from whom you learn or who have otherwise helped you.

Feeling whatever you feel, notice and give thanks to people and other creatures and things that support you.

Act in harmony with your fellow beings, with nature and with inanimate objects.

Fit yourself to the circumstances and situations presented to you by reality.

Know that a thing or an action which may seem of little value to oneself may be a priceless treasure to another.

Consider the perspectives and values of others and learn from them.

Help those who are suffering or disadvantaged and as you yourself become awakened help those who seek to make real their own potential.

Do your best to help others find their constructive lives. Be a model of constructive living for others.

Know that there is no shame in questioning.

Feeling shame or not, ask questions when that is what needs doing.

Be diligent in your practice and on hearing the music of the absolute do not be so foolish as to try to sing its song.

Continue doing what is doable, but don't aim to control the uncontrollable.

Remember to renew the source in order to retain good health.

However well you take care of your body, illness and aging happen. Here, again, do what you can.

Seek neither brilliance nor the void; just think deeply and work hard.

Life satisfaction is likely to accompany a sensible lifestyle and purposeful activity. Pay attention and process the information with care and appreciation.

When still, be as the mountain. When in movement be as the dragon riding the wind.

When you are quiet be fully quiet. When you are in action be fully in action. Act with full attention.

Be aware at all times like the tiger, which only seems to sleep and at all times let the mind be like running water.

Be receptive to input from floating thoughts when necessary; be pinpoint focused when necessary. Train your mind to fit your circumstances.

When you are required to act remember that right motive is essential to right action, just as right thought is essential to right words.

Know your purpose when taking action, verbal or non-verbal. Your actions affect how you think and vice versa.

Beware of creating burdens for yourself or others to carry.

We all cause troubles to others. Become aware of the troubles you cause others, and work to repay them. Awareness leads to both guilt and gratitude for the support received in spite of troubles caused.

Act with necessary distinction being both creative and receptive and transcending subject/object dichotomy.

You "absorb" reality as you interact with it. You take on some characteristics of people with whom you interact. Be aware of this tendency and use it wisely.

Know that you are not the center of the universe but learn to put the universe at your center by accepting the instant of your being.

We tend to interpret reality from our own perspective for our own convenience. Each fresh moment offers the opportunity to interpret as usual or differently.

Seek security within yourself rather than in others.

No therapist or spouse or guru or parent or evangelist can save you. What you do with your life is up to you.

Know that even great worldly wealth and the accumulation of material things are of little worth compared with the priceless treasures: love, peace and the freedom to grow.

Time is not money. Neither is health or life meaning or anything other than money. Money is money. You define your treasures.

Allow yourself to be so that your life may become a time of blossoming.

Keep on doing what needs doing. Do so thoughtfully, gracefully, kindly; losing yourself in each moment.

REFLECTIONS ON THE SAYINGS OF CONFUCIUS

As usual, this writing of reflections is only very loosely related to the original writings of Confucius. I write here about thoughts that occurred to me over a period during which I was reading Confucius' works. I use modern words and modern examples. No translation or interpretation of the original is intended. The ideas here are related to Confucius but closely related to Constructive Living. The basic principles of Constructive Living may be found in the books

Constructive Living and *A Handbook for Constructive Living,* both published by the University of Hawaii Press. Some key differences include Constructive Living's emphasis on the uncontrollability of feelings while remaining responsible for controllable behavior, Constructive Living's recognition that all is borrowed, and Confucius' extensive advice about governing within the Chinese system. Of course there are many similarities in thought. Human wisdom is not dissimilar over time and culture.

It is easier to talk about consistently constructive action than to practice it. Whatever the talk, watch whether clothes are hung up and dishes washed and beds made and appointments kept and promises honored and tools cleaned. Words gust through a house but never become furniture--you can't sit on words.

Don't push your discoveries and beliefs on other people. Make your understanding available and your life exemplary, so that people will ask for your teaching. Those who teach for their own convenience are not teachers; they are thieves. Beware!

Youths watch the behavior of adults. They see what actions are successful and what actions are not. Youths have less to lose than elders, so they are more likely to experiment with behavior. Adults who fail to provide youths with models of successful, constructive actions contribute to youthful delinquency.

You cannot amend your life in the future. You can only change what you do now. You cannot revise your past life. You can only rebuild your past beginning now.

Choose people you respect and admire as friends. Your chances of becoming like them are good. If there are no such people around you either move or live without friends.

Be good without showy goodness. Allow others to be at ease in the presence of your thoughtful kindness.

Your wealth is borrowed; your kindness is borrowed; your life is a hand-me-down. What, then, is the basis for a prideful attitude?

Make promises you can keep, including promises to yourself. Results may be out of your control, so the promises should be structured around what you can do, what you aim for, without promising absolute results.

Speaking a foreign language with little experience requires you to search for words and slow your speech. Select words and pace speech in your native language in similar fashion. Give yourself time to offer your best utterances to others.

Perhaps you didn't ask to be born. Perhaps you aren't asking to die either. In any case, your life is a gift from your parents. You owe them for your life and for the effort they (and/or others) spent feeding and raising you. I am not arguing that they did so perfectly or that your repayment to them will be perfect or that your efforts in behalf of your own children (if you have them) will be perfect. We all row the same sort of boat.

Listen to their speech, but watch what others do, too. It is harder to hide behind deeds than to hide behind words. Others are watching you, too.

Make the effort to praise those who are praiseworthy. Make the effort to thank those who deserve your thanks. Make the effort to notice those who are praiseworthy and "thanksworthy."

Modeling good behavior affects you and others, too. The ripple effect cannot be measured. Brains change.

Carelessness, sloth, and waste are easy. They also have real consequences. Habits become momentary character.

Plain, ordinary depth of character is earned, not inherited. It is borrowed, too. Simple facts.

I can never meet the man who attended that school or raised those children or landed that job or loved that woman or wrote those books. His results keep affecting me now; his existence then must be acknowledged now. Sometimes I wonder about who he/I was. Time's barrier is impenetrable and only reviewed by this mind's filter now. The results of now keep accumulating.

Everything lasts. Perhaps not in the way we wish or expect or even recognize. But setting something in history affects the next moment and the next.

Love prompts wisdom and foolishness, selflessness and selfishness. So keep a careful eye on it (as though you had a choice) and use the information to do good.

Gambling and fashion are ways foolish people make profits from foolish people. Invest your resources meaningfully elsewhere.

Showing strong personal preferences in many areas reveals self-centeredness. Study the preferences of others. Learn to be ordinary. Accept what is. Change what is important.

The imperfections I see in others prompt me to look at my own imperfections…but not enough.

Elderly women represent your mother, and elderly men represent your father. Do what you can for them.

Dying old, isolated, and alone is a sad finale. Get to know your neighbors.

Nagging is misdirected self-examination. What can you do to help?

One way to distract yourself from guilt about not doing what you know needs doing is to flood yourself with more information…reading these reflections, for example.

Beware the foolishness of the fearless, the shallowness of the contented, the narrowness of the pessimist, the pride of the academic, the power of the politician, and the whirlpool of the depressed. Fresh moments keep on coming.

Much power prompts big successes and big failures, friends and enemies.

Clear purposes and straightforward behavior to achieve them are central to Constructive Living. Purposes may be unpopular, but they are your guides to meaningful doing. When your purposes provoke criticism, learn from the criticism. Then you may or may not change your purposes.

Waste diminishes the value of things and inflates the self. Scorn diminishes the value of others and inflates the self. What about pity, cruelty, slander, rudeness, and ridicule? How diligently some people work to keep the self inflated!

Who else sees what you do is unimportant. You see what you do.

Transparency is necessary but not sufficient for good government, good religion, and good citizenship.

Recognize fashion, but you need not yield to it.

Courtesy implies attention to the desires of another person. Courtesy is required, not optional, for a constructive life.

If you try to fix the world or fix your nation or fix your clients or fix your spouse or fix your children you can expect disappointment. You get what you deserve when you act to fix yourself.

Armed forces are not a genuine, long-term solution to any national problem.

Keep an open mind to possibilities while acting on what seems certain based on experience.

Fit yourself to reality's circumstances without expecting the circumstances to fit your desires. Demands reflect lack of reflection.

Fame arrives and flees at its own whim. Reputation is the same. Depend on doing well in any circumstance.

True love is never selfish. Jealousy and domination may try to masquerade as true love, but they are self-centered. You lose yourself in true love, thinking only of the convenience of the loved one.

Don't let possessions possess you. Find imaginative ways to reuse what you own or give away what you no longer use after some set period of time.

Praise the good you see in others. Minimize your complaints to them and about them. Look for the good, even around corners, so you can find more to praise. To do so both encourages good behavior and also encourages praising.

Examine your routine habits now and then. Consider the portions that you eat, your bedtime routine, your traveling, your exercise, your computer and phone habits. Are your purposes clear? Do you need to change anything to fit your purposes better?

Speaking well is an art. In everyday speech choose your words well; use a variety of utterances; be artistic and yet clear in your communications. Electronic communications deserve the same care.

When is enough money enough? When are the latest trendy possessions enough? When do you feel comfortably secure? Desires slip in without invitation. Notice them. Notice supporting and competing purposes, too.

Take pride not in your wealth but in the sources of your wealth.

Capitalism is about finding a bargain, making a profit. Don't let those goals interfere with doing what is right. Don't let rationalizations and excuses for those goals interfere with doing what is right. Store away good deeds safely in the past.

Love is both freeing and restrictive. We escape from the self into caring for the other, but we are exposed to new doubts and worries and fears. New possibilities and new limitations leap forth. While the mind floats keep behavior grounded.

When threatened, preserve your ability to behave kindly. Revenge, however, is a distraction from satisfaction.

Dissatisfaction with yourself is fine; use it to improve. Use worries constructively. Attempts to get rid of self-criticism only show your desire to improve. Praise yourself for self-criticism and upgrade your life's behavior.

Maintain both long-term purposes and immediate purposes. Long-term purposes provide direction, and immediate purposes provide means.

Think less of whether or not a goal is attainable and more about how specifically to attain the goal through behavior.

When forgotten and unknown keep on doing what needs doing. Fame is a trivial byproduct of factors outside of your control. You know when you are doing well; that knowledge is sufficient.

You cannot do everything. Leave some tasks for others. Offer hints to make their doing successful. Credited with your hints or not, you know what you have done. Praise the righteous successes of others.

Upgrade routine and repetitious tasks with attention, novelty, and improvements. Find ways to learn from everyday experience, because everyday experience is not really repeated.

Even those in great power and those in deep poverty have everyday life. No one lives with memorable moments all day every day. Learning to live ordinary everyday life well is worth the effort. You will spend most of your life there.

Aiming to complicate and confuse is unlikely to work as well as explication and simplification. Let reality instruct you; then pass along what you have learned to others.

Don't invest your time in appearing good and fashionable and current. Focus on appearance can distract from more important pursuits.

Conduct government and business affairs with honesty, clarity, and transparency. All true victories are won with integrity no matter what the economic consequences. Feelings of elation or desolation fade over time. The consequences of government and business dealings continue.

Ease your mind with acceptance of what is. Then do what you can to move what is toward what you would like it to be. Then accept the results of your efforts, as desired or not, and do what needs doing next. And so on.

Reading about and talking about and writing about Constructive Living is not the same as doing it; or is it? Do you need more information or more practice? I don't know how to make a constructive life easy, but I do know that the effort is worth it.

So much data is available that the mind works to ignore most of it, attending to what appears to be relevant. Now and then check what sorts of data are being ignored and refine your definitions of relevance. New discoveries await your new purpose.

Punishment is a relatively inefficient way to influence yourself and others. Offer alternate purposes with potential rewards to increase your odds of successful influence.

While repaying debts we incur more debts in endless cycle. Failing to repay also incurs further debts. How fortunate we are to be able to work on our debts while falling behind!

The life lessons you learned in the past are useful. Today new lessons await you. Don't ignore them. Pass along your learned lessons to those who wish to benefit from them.

Keep aware of what you don't know. There is so much unknown out there and in here, so much I will never understand. To have some sense of the boundaries of knowledge is a useful part of knowledge.

It is better to do "ordinary" well most of the time than to try to maintain an image of superiority or holiness all of the time. If your work and income depend on portraying a public image that is different from your off-stage self, then you have sacrificed the benefits of being ordinary. Guarding against discovery is costly. We all face an ordinary end to life, no options.

Breaking the law, even for a righteous cause, incurs a cost. Be ready to pay the price. Be prepared to suffer for doing what you hold to be right even if it appears that you stand alone.

Excesses become boring over time. Topping one's tops becomes more and more difficult over time. A solid baseline of ordinariness makes rare peak moments stand out and facilitates recovery from them.

Keep a record of wisdom wherever you find it, and refer to it now and then. Reminders of wisdom can provide useful discoveries as viewed from changing momentary perspectives.

Find a way to use constructively the brief time between segments, episodes, performances, downloads, etc. Don't "pause" your mind while waiting. When you nap, nap purposefully, not as a default.

Each of us is the convergence of long lines of momentary passion followed by careful attention to the offsprings' needs. We cannot directly repay all of those ancestors. Their representatives are available, however, all around us.

Examples of bad parenting and unkind business practices and grumpy neighbors and thoughtless in-laws and officious officials are wonderful teachers about what not to do. How kind of them! They help us to see ways we can avoid causing trouble to others.

Reflect on the pain and inconvenience your parents went through for you. It matters not at all why they did it. You benefited. Who will reflect on your pain and inconvenience in this way?

There should be no difference between giving your word, your promise, and signing your name to a legal document. So watch your speech with care. What you say is one sign of how you live.

Maintain respectful behavior toward even long-term friends. If you cannot do so there is something wrong with you or your friend or both.

Prepare others to do your work at least as well as you do it. For such preparation you must make your work appealing and give up the notion that nobody else will ever do the work as well as you. Your work, in fact, includes preparing for your departure. How well do you do it?

Stooping to make a friend is stupid. The gaze is misdirected.

Pay attention to detail when it is appropriate, but do not let details dominate you. A variety of purposes are arrayed before you.

The more you receive, the more you have to give away. Notice the two meanings of the words "have to" in the previous sentence. You cannot give away time.

Before throwing something away consider a novel use for it, giving it new life.

It is unnecessary to make excuses for one's virtues. It is unnecessary to boast about them, as well.

When it appears that you are failing miserably you have a good chance to examine your purposes and methods. Great success offers the same opportunity. Be a student of Reality.

Sometimes resting needs to be done. Sometimes waiting (for a computer process to finish, for example) is what needs to be done. While waiting, however, don't turn off your mind.

If you do what you love to do and fail you will have fewer regrets than if you do what you hate to do and fail. The latter involves failing twice.

No human is born with all the knowledge he/she will need. Knowledge must be accumulated thanks to attention and the input from others. Innate capacity may vary, but this truth holds for everyone.

The ordinary is rich with interesting phenomena worth investigating. Don't run after miracles, ghosts, and ephemeral spiritual fantasies.

One who practices good behavior for the convenience of others can afford to be transparent. Liars, fools, and thieves must use energy to maintain their false fronts.

Examine the purposes underlying your actions. When the purpose for an action is clear, then you need not examine it again unless the situation changes. Do not act impulsively or randomly, without purpose.

Confucius considered himself imperfect, failing to consistently live up to his own standards. All of the humans you idolize are like that. Accept your inability to consistently live up to your own standards. Do what you can to do so anyway.

Social expectations help guide us and keep us in line. Such expectations are not absolute, however. When your purpose is clear and right you need not behave in socially expected ways. When a custom is unconstructive yet thoughtlessly followed, embody an example of a better custom.

It takes time to develop a constructive life. Several years of carefully applying constructive life principles usually leads to a solid grounding in constructive habits. Such habits, too, need polishing.

Be observant and ready to see new angles, new interpretations, new possibilities. A closed mind bores itself with safety concerns.

Knowing wisdom you have the responsibility to pass it on to others but not the right to force it on others. You learn not only for your own sake. Leak your discoveries. Allow circumstances to be your teachers, not your excuses.

Like a flowing stream life keeps happening. Don't think that one event stops the stream and must be resolved for the stream to move on.

It isn't necessary to feel like writing or paying bills or fixing the brakes or washing the dishes. Just do what needs doing while floating along on the stream.

The possibilities and potential of youth are worth nothing unless nurtured by diligent action. Dreams must be actualized with effort.

Young or old we must find ways to pay on the borrowed debt of our existence. Offering information, giving a smile, waiting for another to go first, turning off a forgotten light, picking up trash, greeting a stranger—such acts are available to most of us.

Principles can be memorized. Applying principles in daily life requires attention and focusing in on detail.

Spread too much jam on your toast and it gets on your fingers and drips down on the table. Know the right amounts of things and efforts.

Fit your speech and movements and attire to the circumstance unless you have a purpose that includes drawing attention to the unusual.

Show respect to others whether you feel it or not, but not overly. We are all humans. We all represent Reality.

The ads in Buddhist magazines tell us about Buddhism in America. Perhaps someday sanghas will announce the size of their donation pool, the breadth of their holdings, the value of their properties (rather like the television game shows that announce big prizes in order to establish their worth.) Books, retreats, centers, and individuals announce their ability to guide the seeker toward some sort of earned bliss, for a price. The show goes on.

Make no attempt to appear calm and composed all the time. When startled, be startled; when sad, be sad; when angry, be angry. Whatever feelings appear on your face, remain the good steward of controllable actions.

Too much effort can cause trouble just as too little effort. Trying to find the perfect sleeping position can lead to insomnia. Trying to write the perfect novel may lead to never submitting a manuscript for publication. Too many facial reconstructions can lead to ugliness. Reasonable purposes and proper effort maximize chances for success.

Enthusiasm, like any feeling, comes and goes. Use it when it is helpful. Nevertheless, don't allow it to lead you in directions you don't wish to go.

When the time comes to retire from a business or anything else, do so. Then turn to what needs doing next.

However grounded you may be there will be moments of anxiety, fear, and self-doubt. Scan the feelings for the information they hold for you. Make no attempt to vanquish them. They are natural elements of the situation you are in, as you are. What needs doing next?

Dictatorship conceals itself in many forms. When citizens fear the government, when citizens mistrust the government, when citizens fail to see the government supporting them, then beware of a concealed dictatorship. Don't be fooled by the superficial facade of government.

Experiment by giving beyond the demands of someone who demands too much from you. See if your proactive giving changes your attitude.

The ideal is to have no need for laws and courts and lawyers. The reality is that all people are not good all of the time. Do your part to make laws unnecessary. Knowing what is good to do is not the same as practicing it. Praise the good actions of others.

You don't cause others to steal, but your covetous behavior encourages them. Where accumulating wealth is the main game in town some will try to cheat in order to win.

Being well-known is not the same as being worthy. To be both is rare.

Confucius is quoted in Chapter XXI-3. "'If doing what is to be done be made the first business, and success a secondary consideration;-- is not this the way to exalt virtue?" In Constructive Living terms "Do what needs to be done. Results are uncontrollable."

When necessary give advice, but don't be attached to the outcome. Scan to consider whether the advice you are about to give applies to yourself as well.

Be careful in speech. Your speech influences your thinking and the thinking of those who hear it. Speak clearly with clear purpose.

The theory is that laws curb human excesses. However, thieves break them, and the powerful and wealthy amend them in their favor. When individual purposes reflect the convenience of others rather than the self, then there is surer footing for curbing human excesses.

When we hurry we are unlikely to act thoroughly. When we act from habit, without attention, we are unlikely to act thoroughly. When possible, take time to slow down and attend to the details of everyday activities.

Being cautious prevents some mistakes. But caution alone inhibits progress toward other goals. Mix caution with exploration.

Flattery is unnecessary, but find the good in others.

You can't please everyone; so don't try. Sometimes you don't please anyone; so hold to your purpose. When you don't please yourself change your purposes and behavior.

Economic goals are not ultimate. They may explain some behavior but not all behavior. Recognize your economic situation and respond to it, but do not be pushed around by it.

Fame is a by-product. Going for it as a primary goal is a mistake. Find something to do that you do very well.

Government that uses language to cover reality instead of revealing reality must be corrected. News reporting is the same. Beware of repetitious standard, bland talk about standard, bland subjects.

Hype is purposeful lying. Beware!

You may seek advice about a problem, but the effort to change your behavior and the credit for changing your behavior is yours.

The problem with justice is that the powerful usually define it. Be aware of the law. Then do what is unselfish and right.

You don't always get what you deserve. Accept the rough times, too, and learn from them how to do differently and better.

When government becomes obsessed with spinning words, then its attention is misdirected from governing properly. When laws are minutely framed by legalistic terms then attention has been misdirected from justice.

Hold yourself to the same standards that you hold others. Demand more from yourself than you demand from others, then carry through on your expectations of self.

Be ready for new perspectives, new discoveries, new interpretations. Fresh moments encourage alertness.

Our desires outpace our achievements and our possessions. Good imaginations create more desires and dissatisfaction with what is already ours. Praise, don't vainly resist, your imagination, and get on with doing what needs to be done. Desires offer more information, not sure guidelines.

Social recognition for your life depends on many factors outside of your control. It is fine to do well while unrecognized.

Beware when the media (or a social group) consistently praises or vilifies someone. Look deeper to find the human within the projected image.

The speed of light is truth. Our talk about it, even our equations describing it, are not the same sort of truth. Truth is beyond reliability.

I can suggest something for you to do. However, ultimately, you decide what you need to do. Reality will give you feedback when your behaviors are foolish or evil or ill-considered. Then do something different. Reality will give you feedback when your behaviors are wise or merely sufficient. Then do what needs doing next.

Beware stories about why people do what they do, whether the stories be scholarly or magical or religious or commonsense. Actions are observable, but motivations are not. Too many variables are involved. Nevertheless, we are all prone to create and believe explanatory stories.

The words you speak to others are gifts. Choose them carefully. Watch the reactions of others to your words. Then speak carefully again, if necessary.

Worthy of awe are three things: Reality exists, I exist in Reality, you exist in Reality. Put simply, Reality is awesome.

Your feelings of anger have no direct effect on others around you. What you do (your behavior) related to your anger has much effect on others around you. Whatever you feel be careful about your behavior. Therein lies responsibility.

When you think you have mastered something Reality is ready to teach you otherwise. When you think you know it all, you are simply wrong. When you think you know how much you don't know, you are wrong again. Keep on learning.

Following custom is not necessarily right or safe. Know your purpose.

The more you possess, the more you must store and protect. Don't let possessions possess you.

Deceit requires hidden purposes and careful memory and misleading behavior. Deceit is wasteful of effort and energy.

Perhaps you worry about growing old and becoming dependent on other people for your everyday living needs. Perhaps you failed to notice that you are already dependent on others for these needs whether you are six or sixteen or twenty-six or forty-six or any other age. No one ever lives independently.

People are not tissues to be used and discarded. People are like flowers to be nurtured and treasured.

Places are tools, too. Places make tasks easier or harder. Use place and time with attention.

Those who divide their lives into small tasks and large tasks are in error. There are no small tasks. Attend well to the buttoning of a shirt and the closing of a drawer and the emptying of a wastebasket. The practice will do you well when other tasks appear.

Mourning reminds us to take good care of those who are still living.

Pessimistic predictions sometimes turn out to be accurate. But holding long-term pessimism has its price.

Expectations of perfection in self or others are unrealistic. Moments of perfection may be possible.

These words float on the surface and appear scenic. Under these words are currents that are not readily visible. Few will dive deeply to sense the strength of the underlying flow.

Money, too, is a tool for accomplishing your purposes and repaying debts of all sorts. All money is borrowed, like the means by which you earned it and the opportunities to spend it.

Demands see others as tools; requests see others as humans. Which do you prefer? When there are explanations and personal benefits for acquiescing to a request there is more incentive to cooperate. After consideration, social benefits may be seen as personal benefits.

How am I different from ages twenty to seventy? For one thing, I treasure and take better care of the people and things that help me accomplish purposes I take better care of my body, my work tools, other humans, my clothing, my car, my furniture, and whatever else comes to hand.

Yin Chih Wen, The Tract of the Quiet Way

(Original translated by Teitaro Suzuki and Paul Carus. [1906].)

Here again I nibble at the edges of wisdom, suggesting more modern, Constructive Living interpretations and associated thoughts. I suggest that you go to the ancient Taoist work in order to see the extensions here.

Life satisfaction comes from wisdom-based purposes and action, not from avoiding unpleasant feelings and aiming for lots of fun.

Whether your good deeds are recognized or not, keep doing what you believe is right.

Consider the convenience of others, including all things living and inanimate.

Habits of goodness or anything else are developed by repeated practice.

Dishonesty requires sustained effort, remembering, and self-deception.

Being in government allows the opportunity to work on debts to those governed.

Notice the details of your circumstances and apply your effort thoughtfully.

What do you owe your dishes and your keys and your phone and your toothbrush? Does kindness require awareness?

Weigh distrust and anger against debt and obligation. Be civil in your service.

Religious beliefs (including atheism) are grammars. They vary in the degree to which they accurately describe shared reality. Free speech does not excuse harming others.

However carefully we aim to describe realistic living our words are landlocked by self. Beware attempts to sail absolute passenger ships on land.

Offer your assistance but do not require it. Be available without intrusion. Each person must save himself or herself. Don't hinder the process by intrusive helpfulness.

Compassion may follow giving to those in need. It need not precede the giving.

Recommend wise people (including authors) and wise Internet sites to others. Offer wisdom in your electronic and other communications. Don't steal others' time and attention with trivia.

Use your possessions carefully; then recycle as much as possible. You will merely be returning borrowed objects.

Explore details of what loved ones want done with their possessions when they die. Let them know what you want done with your possessions. Use your death as an opportunity to work on your debts.

Contribute your resources to efforts that encourage humans to live well.

True education is not business; true education is not based on economics. Current institutional myths devalue education just as current institutional myths devalue religion. Beware handicapping noble pursuits by means of financial objectives.

Your resources (including time) are all borrowed. Share them first with those you know, so you can see direct results of your sharing. Then extend to others in need.

Be a careful consumer. Know relative prices and qualities. Use money well, neither hoarding wealth nor overspending. Share your experiences of goods and services with others.

Treat customers, employees, and employers with consideration. Learn from them about your own strengths and imperfections.

Find ways to make wisdom public. Update your communications with realistic content.

Volunteer to support the poor, the sick, and the elderly. Minimize your own need for public welfare support.

Use solar energy when feasible. Support handicap access projects. (For example, the original of The Tract of the Quiet Way is "Light lanterns in the night to illuminate where people walk. Keep boats on rivers to ferry people across.")

Prevent unwanted breeding of pets. Support animal shelters

We kill living creatures in order to eat. Directly by butchering and indirectly through pesticides and radiators of delivery trucks and antibacterial chemicals and fumigation and hand washing we kill living creatures. Edible plants are living creatures, too. No one survives without the sacrifice of life. So we are obligated to use those sacrifices thoughtfully, with appreciation of the gifts and minimal waste.

While walking be mindful of the convenience of automobile drivers and children at play and other pedestrians and crawling insects. Walking, too, offers the opportunity to work on your debts.

Electricity and fire befriend us with possibilities. Don't turn them into enemies through carelessness and inattention.

Select your environmental concerns carefully. See that your actions reflect your beliefs in this area.

Keep your car and all tools maintained. Thank them for their service whether they can hear or not; the thanking is for you, too.

Find new uses for objects you have used already. Donate those that others could reuse.

Do not compete with others for more things and more expensive things. If you must compete, challenge yourself to use the possessions you have more wisely and unselfishly.

Envy is uncontrollable directly by your will. Use it to stimulate yourself to work harder to achieve your noble purposes.

Do not sacrifice others in your own goal achievement. In love or business or recreation or the arts consider first the convenience of others.

Lawsuits encompass more than money awards. Consider the extensive time and attention required before undertaking or prompting one. Alternate solutions are often possible.

Our very existence causes trouble to those around us. Directly or indirectly they provide us with food and clothing and transportation and shelter and more. They must take us into consideration when walking and driving and conversing and making change and creating products and manufacturing them and making laws and so forth. We are fortunate to continue to benefit from their efforts in our behalf. Remember to thank and repay as much as possible.

If you must listen, listen directly to both sides of a quarrel. CL assignments include thanking the quarreling other ten times a day for specific services and doing secret services for the benefit of him or her.

Stimulating others to quarrel and blame and criticize injures your own reputation eventually.

The wealthy and powerful die, too. Use your authority with this truth in mind. Your Internet influence is ephemeral. Your actions have lasting effects.

What do you do with your wealth? How do you invest your resources? Are your purposes other than self-serving?

No one is "self-made". All success contains elements of the efforts of others. Humility is simply realistic.

Getting along with others makes life easier for all of us. Getting along is a resource you can give others regardless of your economic status.

Hatred happens. Like all feelings you cannot will it away. However, you need not let it spur your actions. While hating, do what is kind and just.

It is quite common to become like those with whom you spend time. So choose friends and lovers carefully.

If you regularly do what is clearly right, then you will find no need to obsess over the gray areas of right and wrong.

No deliberate lies are little or white.

Refer to wise writing now and then, and recall the words you read.

Sloppy speech and writing generates sloppy thinking. Use your language as a tool for developing your mind. Choose words carefully.

Make hiking paths clearer for those who hike after you. Make roads clear of debris. Make driving easier for fellow drivers. Make tasks easier for fellow workers. Make your job easier for those who replace you. Put your home in good shape for new buyers. Find better, clearer ways to teach others.

Find creative ways to do everyday personal tasks. Innovate at work. Find new ways to say something you have uttered hundreds of times before.

Support others in their efforts to support others. Expand peacemaking and rehabilitation through modeling and contributions.

Live so that others can perceive constructive life principles in your behavior. Do so without intimidation so that others seek to emulate your behavior. While being exemplary be ordinary.

Make your wisdom available to others through speech and writing and other media.

You have a sense of what is good and kind behavior. Consider the convenience of others when acting.

Life has no time-out until death. Fill your waking moments with attention to the situational details and purposes and behaviors of a constructive life. Build creatively on your accumulated wisdom. Don't turn off your mind while sweeping or hanging up clothes or filling the gas tank.

Be alert during your pre-sleep routine. Prepare for sleep in an orderly fashion. Then accept the uncontrollability of sleep's emergence.

Bad habits begin with a single behavior. Bad character begins with bad habits. Emphasize building flexible, good habits rather than avoiding bad ones. Results are not perfectly controllable, but good results are more likely with proper action. Each moment presents the opportunity to do what fits the situation.

Thoughts and felt emotions do not directly affect the external world. Behaviors are visible, affecting the external and internal worlds. All affects are lasting, even when appearing minimal. Behaviors cannot be excised from the past.

Countless efforts of others occur in your behalf. They made the screen you use to read this work. They provided the genes that allowed your eyes to see this screen. They taught you how to read. Their products and services give you time and energy to make sense of what you read. No matter how much you paid, it is never equal to these accumulating benefits.

Of course, all these benefits come to me, too. Nothing special. Ordinarily overwhelmed.

REFLECTIONS ON PASCAL'S PENSEES

As you may expect by now, my reflections sometimes range far from the material that prompts them. You are invited to go to the original (*Pensees*, in this case) to discover how far. Find more "Reflections" on the http://constructiveliving.org and www.constructiveliving2.weebly.com websites.

Some people who encounter Constructive Living intuitively understand many of the principles immediately. Others seem to need much time and repeated challenging of the principles before acknowledging their validity. Constructive Living does not require faith and obedience, as in religions. We simply recommend that you compare Constructive Living suggestions with your own experience. Adopt only the parts of Constructive Living that make sense to you based on your life experience. These days there is much information propounded as psychological common sense that just isn't realistic. Build your own understanding of the workings of the human mind based on the workings of your own mind in daily life, not based upon what some supposed expert in psychology tells you is so.

I'll make effort to write in a style that is interesting and clear. But don't be fooled by style. Continue to evaluate the contents. No one suggests that living by Constructive Living principles is easy; only that it is practical and realistic. You will avoid some unnecessary suffering and misplaced effort by practicing Constructive Living, but there will continue to be plenty of ordinary misery and confusion in your life whatever you do. There is no supernatural magic here.

Wisdom is accumulated and borrowed. Sometimes we recognize the source of wisdom, sometimes it just appears as a gift. It may go unrecognized. Stay alert! One test of wisdom is that no matter how diligently and imaginatively we attack it, wisdom remains unconquered. It outlasts our finest weapons.

Knowing when to talk, how much to talk, and how to talk well requires a kind of intuitive skillful style that is developed, if at all, over time. I talk too much and write too little. As I edit my writing I learn the limitations of my speech.

Pascal and Morita held that our minds are constructed so that when presented with an idea we are likely to think of its opposite. Thus, we are natural skeptics. So, of course, I begin to think of exceptions to the previous generalization. Then exceptions to the exceptions, and so forth. Having no great interest in discovering how far my mind is willing to pursue this foolishness, I turn to something else.

Mentally playing with ideas is a relatively safe pastime, provided the game doesn't interfere with doing life with appropriate, purposeful behavior. Mental "wheelspinning" may be a poor substitute for visiting the sick or writing the report or swinging the bat.

Psychological research can, at best, illuminate bare edges of the mind. Anyone who thinks he understands the human mind (with his own mind, no less!) is foolishly grandiose. Minds operate in ways far beyond our ability to measure and understand them. Knowing our grand limitations, we will not give up our study of the mind. Minds will continue studying minds. Reality seeks to reveal itself.

Reason is stories made up about why. I have no objection to being reasonable, provided there are no associated claims to justice or absolute correctness or victory.

Education produces new discoveries and perspectives while producing blind spots and prejudices. Every education-moment involves a preferred perspective on phenomena. Here, too. There is no way to view reality from all perspectives. Each perspective is itself a created element of ever-renewing reality.

Imagination creates both art and misery. Science without imagination is dull, lacking progress. There is no neurosis without active imagining. Neither good nor bad, imagination depends on its uses. It deserves praise or rebuke depending on its use in the moment. Creator of possibilities, imagination adds color to already colorful reality.

The you-now may resemble the you-of-last-week or the-you-of-yesterday in looks and habits, but you are really a new creature. Each moment offers you the opportunity to change. Only the words look alike.

To know one's calling is a blessed privilege. To discover what one is meant to do in life requires both a search and the prodding of good fortune. Effort polishes this gem. Details are resolved in hindsight. Lean into it.

We tend to look for information that supports what we already believe. We feel some degree of upset when we must diverge from our preferred thought patterns. Steady familiarity may appear safe and comfortable, but reality won't permit it for long.

Some people try to hide all their faults. Others reveal some faults in order to conceal others they find more despicable. Hiding faults for the convenience of self is different from hiding faults for the convenience of others. In real life, often the intentions are mixed. Remember that you have the right to define what are your faults.

The easy course is to believe deceptions as true, both the deceptions of others and our own deceptions. When words deceive, then observe non-verbal behavior to discover the truth. It is harder to lie with our non-verbal behavior than with words.

"Time heals grief and quarrels, for we change and are no longer the same persons," wrote Pascal. Feelings fade. We change. No surprise here, just ordinary human wisdom. How then can we speak of national character, of Arabs, of Jews, of Americans, of Japanese, of eternal love, of never-ending fear?

When I underwent a week of absolute isolated bedrest to experience one of the techniques of Japan's Morita therapy, I understood the unnaturalness of inactivity. My body longed to be actively engaged in some meaningful, purposeful pursuit. Complete dependency on others for all my needs being met produced both gratitude and unease. It was difficult to endure the full week, especially the long nights and days during which sleep was difficult after my body was so rested.

Whatever the results, the doing is important.

When all goes well, the shink (momentary neurotic person) wonders why and how long it will last. When things go poorly, the shink forgets the good times and perceives life as always having been this way. Thus, both anticipation and memory work to sustain misery for the shink.

At some point many of us surpass the amount of the possessions necessary for our basic needs, and the possessions begin to possess us. Social science research shows that after a certain basic level of possessions are obtained, adding to those possessions does not increase happiness. You know that storing things and finding things and protecting things and preserving things and efforts to keep up with fashion and payments and image all create worry and effort. Accumulating more and more weighs heavier and heavier. Know the difference between necessity and greed. Consume wisely. The consumer is never king, often serf. If you think that you already know such truth but don't act on it, then you are more foolish than those who first encounter it here.

Find something useful, purposeful to do. Then find something useful, purposeful to do. And so forth. Play can be useful and purposeful, too. However, a mix of activities is easier to sustain, and more interesting.

It is not surprising that we feel some pride when others praise us. However, to do praiseworthy deeds in order to receive praise from others is misdirected purpose. Furthermore, the praise may or may not come; it is uncontrollable. Better to do praiseworthy deeds because they need doing. Making a show of trying to hide one's good deeds is misplaced effort that could better be directed toward more good deeds.

Tomorrows keep reemerging and yesterdays keep piling up. Today has available moments right now. Uh-oh, there it went, but here comes another one. How are you using it? As you know, the nows don't come endlessly. Clocks can be synchronized, but your now and my now are never exactly the same.

Doubts help make the world interesting, adding dimensions of meaning to the ordinary. Doubts also interfere with simple, comfortable interpretations of reality. In any case, doubts happen to us. Aiming to suppress them in self or others is unrealistic. Just notice them for the information they contain and go on to what needs doing next.

The one who will die is not me-now. That fellow may have my name and a body that resembles mine now, but he is not me-now. This me-now is alive and writing. He will have disappeared when you read these words. For all my neurotic anxiety anticipating my death, I-now know nothing about it.

Limits surround us. We cannot break through some of them no matter what degree our wealth or knowledge or popularity or righteousness. Recognizing which barriers cannot be breached and accepting them without useless effort to break through them makes for sensible living. Recognizing which barriers to push against with some chance of success adds interest to living. You cannot fly merely by flapping your arms, but you can sail your mind.

Science keeps turning magic into reason. Meanwhile, science's observation effects turn reason into magic. From where I stand I cannot know with complete objectivity, only from where I stand. Okay, that will have to do. Magical knowledge is less verifiable than scientific knowledge. Both, however, suffer from problems of replication.

Belief, like feelings, happens to you. You can increase the likelihood of belief, like any feeling, by what you do. Reading scripture, talking with believers, attending services, praying, and so forth may stimulate religious faith. But belief cannot be turned on and off by decision. Avoiding religious belief is influenced, too, by what you do. Your faith in gravity has been supported by many acts and results. By the way, choices happen to you, too.

What beliefs should you encourage by your actions? My first suggestion is that you expose yourself to a wide variety of beliefs, not only those of your own culture but also those of cultures quite different from your own. Becoming aware of the variety of accepted beliefs provides perspective on those you hold, and those that hold you. Examine and clarify your beliefs in detail. Evaluate the beliefs by holding them to the light of your own life experience. Don't be convinced by abstract authority, but allow the suggestions of those you trust to have some evaluative weight. Be aware of changing beliefs; beliefs must fit life situations. Act so as to encourage realistic beliefs. Doubts, too, are beliefs; act so as to encourage realistic doubts.

For the constructive life it is not a matter of acting on feelings or acting on reason. Both feelings and reason offer information. Using both forms of information to generate purposeful action is the constructive course.

Our minds can leap beyond what we can see and touch. As much as possible, aim to find ways to validate possibilities with your own senses, your own experience. Both science and religion require some trust in the reports of others' sensory experiences. You cannot perform all scientific experiments yourself. You cannot have all moments of spiritual enlightenment. Be careful whom you trust.

You choose what needs to be done. You decide what is right and just. My hope is that enough of us select values of righteousness and justice that a constructive society is possible. I must be careful to avoid equating my values with those of a constructive society. Reality shows us what works and what doesn't. As Pascal put it, "Can anything be more ridiculous than that a man should have the right to kill me because he lives on the other side of the water, and because his ruler has a quarrel with mine, though I have none with him?" Laws and policies are made by people with power and authority. Unjust and unfair laws may be broken in service of what you consider right and just, but be prepared to pay the consequences of breaking them.

I am not the same person who wrote all those books long ago. I can tell you intimate stories about that person who wrote them. I continue to receive royalties from some of those books as well as borrowed respect and Internet blogs and email thanks to those books. As my memory and body change, so does this me. I learned long ago not to depend on others' evaluations of my momentary success. Recognition came and went and came and went frivolously, well outside of my control. I could only have some degree of control over my doing, my writing, for example. Even then the ideas for writing needed reading and time to stimulate their appearance.

People with little to lose can afford to take great risks. Those in power would do well to pass along to the populace so much that the satisfaction with a good life would deter the risk of rebellion. Everyone wins.

Traffic lights don't change just for me, and planes don't fly safely because I am aboard. Yet my perspective colors all that I perceive. Even when I try to take on the perspective of others, it is from my perspective of their perspectives.

The experience of tasting chocolate is not the same as the chemicals in chocolate or the synapses flashing in tongue and brain. Of course, all are related, but not the same. Similarly, spoken words and the ideas "behind" them are related, but they are not the same.

Laws are made by and for those in power. Do not ignore laws. Then, without doing harm to others, without thinking only of your own convenience, do what you need to do.

Although we are not skeptical of our skepticism we may be proud of our pride and ignorant of our ignorance.

The satisfaction that comes from doing a secret service for another is a natural result of virtuous behavior. The desire to have the secret discovered with resulting social appreciation is a rather common side effect.

Of course, what you think you need to do may not be what others think you need to do. That discrepancy is information for your consideration, not to be ignored. Nevertheless, your behavior is your responsibility.

Losing what you once had brings your attention to its worth. You may not notice the value of something you never had. Then, again, imagination may even inflate value beyond its realistic worth.

Reason does not fight against emotions; reason fights against reason's interpretation of emotions. Emotions are just fine as they are, even when there are conflicting emotions.

If there is a God, then we know about that God thanks to that God's efforts in our behalf. Breakfast appears on the table thanks to the efforts of others, even for the one who prepares it. These written words are the same. Those who think their thoughts are their own are mistaken; even their mistaken thoughts are borrowed. Such a perspective is not scientific because it is not subject to disproof. Science may be respected, but it will never be the religion of the future. All I can say with confidence is that thinking happens.

Of course, illness and death are inevitable. Our minds will decline, and our bodies will lose youthful beauty. Given that future (or present), it is important to use the now well. Dwelling on inevitability doesn't get the lawn raked or the soup made.

To say that evil is in the eye of the beholder puts evil in one's own eye for saying so. And so it is.

I see myself as the center of the universe. Each of us does so. We can abstractly entertain the notion that others think as we do, but for all our attempts at empathy we cannot see as though through the eyes of another. The universe is filled with individual centers.

What Pascal calls "willing what God wills" is much like what we call "accepting reality as it is" in Constructive Living. That path seems the most reasonable one to life satisfaction.

Pascal wrote, "471. It is unjust that men should attach themselves to me, even though they do it with pleasure and voluntarily. I should deceive those in whom I had created this desire; for I am not the end of any, and I have not the wherewithal to satisfy them. Am I not about to die? And thus the object of their attachment will die." I, too, have worked hard to expose my foolishness to those who might seek to attach to some sort of superior being. I am merely a means by which some information gets out into the world. Constructive Living is no more than common human wisdom formatted into words understandable in this place and time. Don't be fooled!

Pascal goes overboard in his ranting about hating the self, unworthiness of receiving love, and depravity of will. It is the static quality of the argument that fails. He misses our changeableness from moment to moment, including the dynamic nature of emotions and actions. Sometimes this, sometimes that. Like all of us much of the time, he sees what he looks for. He reads as though he were trying to convince God that he fully believed that original sin idea. Then in the 480's his argument begins to sound somewhat like the Constructive Living notion that we deserve self-esteem only in that Reality deserves esteem and we are part of that Reality.

Those who believe that Constructive Living is a simple bringing together of Morita therapy and Naikan therapy from Japan clearly don't know either Morita therapy or Naikan therapy well. Constructive Living has extended and molded the theories and practice to create something beyond those origins. Constructive Living fits both East and West. Now Constructive Living has its own history.

Pascal's "It is better not to fast, and be thereby humbled, than to fast and be self-satisfied therewith" appears noble at first. Look again. It discourages what he considers right action and misses the reality that the occurrence of self-satisfaction is outside of our control. Constructive Living recommends that you go ahead and give to the poor, speak kindly to others, recycle your trash and so on. After doing so, if you feel self-satisfaction or not, the results of your actions are safely tucked away in history.

Receiving praise or blame is uncontrollable. Achieving the results you desire from behavior is uncontrollable. Do what is right and appropriate to the situation anyway. Thus, you stay within the area of your control. Everything you do matters.

These writings will make a great deal of sense to some, and not to others. Just as Yoshimoto couldn't predict who would do deep Naikan, I have no idea who will put these suggestions into daily practice. Anyway, I must write; it needs to be done.

Those who point out our faults deserve our thanks, just as those who praise us. Their words may cause us to consider and change what we do, but there is no obligation to do so.

Some humans are blind and know they are blind. Others are blind but think they can see. Most humans are sometimes blind, sometimes not. Did you ever lose the sunglasses that were pushed up on your head?

There are no trivial tasks, only this task now.

Comparing yourself with your fantasy about anyone else is meaningless. Comparing yourself with your guess about what you might have been is meaningless. Comparing yourself with your vision of what you might become is meaningless. All such comparisons are like looking out of a stadium though a keyhole.

Reality doesn't hide itself from those who don't see. One need not be a chosen seeker to see what is there. One needs only to look (or listen, touch, and so forth).

Scientific understanding of the details of the workings of Reality doesn't diminish its macro and micro magnificence. That circumstances work in lawful ways displays a wondrous order to this world. However, science doesn't provide either the only explanation or a complete explanation for the workings of Reality.

Human wisdom has a longer lifespan than human laws. Fashion, economics, and political pressures are among the factors that force change in human laws. However, human wisdom makes sense across cultures and times. In the process of translating Japanese psychotherapies into Western terms I discovered human wisdom.

Again, always test these writings against your own experience. They exist as just another aspect of reality for your information, helpful or not in determining what you need to do.

When we first see a magic trick we may be puzzled, but after it is explained we find it hard to fail to see how it was done. When we first hear a foreign language it just a cacophony of sounds, but after we learn that language we cannot return to the sounds without meaning. Once the Constructive Living way of thinking and acting becomes familiar it becomes harder to ignore the Constructive Living perspective on the fresh moments of your life.

"To understand the meaning of an author, we must make all the contrary passages agree," wrote Pascal (684). I would be surprised if this statement were true of any author, especially me. We change; a sort of inconsistency is ordinary. Again, think not of a static person, but of a dynamic person-situation fit.

Make enough predictions and some are likely to come true. Forget the misses and remember the hits and you are likely to believe in your predictive skills. Anticipating the future is ordinary. Believing in special powers of foretelling the future is unrealistic.

Simple writing is not always easy. Simple doing is not always simple or easy. Forming habits of behavior can lead to simplification and ease, but the forming process itself is not likely to be simple or easy.

Flowers bloom even when I'm not looking. I walk along breathing miracles. Unnoticed, ordinary miracles suffuse me.

Most often we see what we expect to see. The price of quick recognition is blindness elsewhere. Practice looking for the unusual, the hidden secrets of everyday life.

Making effort to see through the eyes of an enemy reveals more similarities than differences. Humans are much more alike than different. To participate in a fight you have to cooperate. No one can fight another person alone. Turning away keeps you out of a fight.

The mind cannot be reduced to electrical firing in the brain, and yet study of the electrical firing in the brain can help us understand the mind to some degree.

Those people you don't know well may be considered saints or devils. Those people you know intimately have more human characteristics. Beware admiration from a distance. We humans are very much alike.

Certainty in self and experts is soothing. However, the more we know the less absolute our trust in certainty becomes. Nevertheless, it is wise to recognize the likely odds.

Rebels may not be correct, but they may be interesting for their fresh alternatives. They, too, do what they see needs to be done. Diversity enables evolution (and folly).

Humans and dogs may obey rules without understanding their purpose. Humans, however, more readily and more contentedly obey rules when they understand the reasonable purposes underlying them.

Teachers have a special responsibility to live the truths they teach. We are all teachers, wittingly or unwittingly. Who learns from you? How do they learn?

REFLECTIONS OF SELF—THOUGHTS ON THE IMITATION OF CHRIST

I select for reflection the writings from a variety of religious thinkers because they were concerned with the workings of the mind long before there was a discipline of psychology. While reading The Imitation of Christ my thoughts wander sometimes in opposite directions from Thomas A. Kempis. As usual, my reflections are not interpretations or translations of the stimulating text, and they are often only tangentially connected at all.

It's hard to get it right

Every time.

So we don't.

But giving up

Is no solution either.

We do what we can.

There is so much we don't know; so why pretend to know a lot? Better to be seen as a seeker of knowledge than a possessor of it. Experts are tools used by management and media. The best experts know their limits.

The better you know yourself, the better you know everything else. The mystery of self-mastery lies in unmasking this dichotomy.

Names and knowledge get passed along for a while, but they are absorbed or forgotten over time. However costly, wisdom is not a private possession.

Striving for status

Makes walls and traps.

Count on dying someday

Buried with or without awards.

Your effort is borrowed, too.

Be a path, not a billboard.

Evaluate carefully the news you read and hear. Evaluate carefully the news that arises from your feelings and thoughts. Make sure the news is worthy before acting upon it. Pass along news that is helpful and uplifting and as truthful as you can determine. Ensure that your own life is newsworthy in the sense that it is helpful and uplifting and full of truth.

Don't waste your time quibbling about the fine points of this writing. Use what you find useful. No one knows the true source of this writing, including its author. The pain of others is a word, "pain", but your pain is different. Words are only word-reality; you cannot drink "coffee". The words you read here are only as useful as you use them.

Keep clear the distinction between uncontrollable feelings and controllable behavior. Work on your behavior while acknowledging thoughts and feelings. Carry responsibility for what you do no matter what you feel.

Don't expect perfection from yourself or anyone else. Rather, expect occasional disappointment to be natural. However, the disappointment is far outweighed by the successes and gains so often taken for granted. Take notice of the achievements endowed upon you and others. To take great pride in one's achievements is to ignore the obvious.

However hard you work to create and maintain a pleasing and healthy face and body you cannot be assured of living even beyond today. Sickness happens. Friends die. Houses are leveled by catastrophe. This moment is a valuable gift. Health happens. Friends support us. Houses protect us. Those who ignore such bequests feel unnecessary misery.

Choose your partners, companions, and workmates wisely. You risk becoming like them. Choose those who share noble purposes and thoughtful behavior. Your values, and the values of those around you, should be well-considered and well-molded into habits of behavior. They need not be the same as the taken-for-granted values of your society. Be ready to pay the price for doing what you believe is right. Family relationships, patriotism, and personal debts of any sort do not obviate your responsibility for doing what is right.

No matter how much authority you have in society, no matter how much power you have in business, you are subject to the vagaries of Reality. Your body will remind you of limitations. Others will evade your attempts to control. You will have moments of doubt and despair. You will die. You will spend much of your time eating, sleeping, defecating, washing, dressing, and moving your body from place to place just as we all do. Medicine may be useful at times, but medicine will not save you. Money may be useful at times, but money will not save you. Religion may be useful at times, but religion will not save you. Education may be useful at times, but education will not save you. Family may be supportive at times, but family will not save you. Be alert to use the moments you have been granted; use them well. Whatever your position and title, you are just this moment's mind/body in action.

Life would be simpler if everyone agreed with your opinions and preferences, simpler but boring. Look for the truth in opinions that differ from yours. Learn from objections and criticism. Such effort will untrack the gut response of anger. Considered anger is much preferable to blind anger. We aren't as clever as we think we are. And others may be sharper than we thought.

Perhaps if you watch enough television and cinema you will begin to believe that at any moment of your everyday life some startling event will take place. The odds are against it. So you would do well to refine the routines of your everyday life so that satisfaction is maximized. Don't wait for good fortune or disaster to strike you. Use this moment well. Don't throw away your words in idle gossip. Your conversation can be a gift offered to others while aligning your own mind positively.

As we grow older more attention turns to our bodies. Health and illness increasingly become topics in our conversations. Tasks that were simple in the past require more attention and effort to accomplish. Sometimes our lives seem to go into fast forward mode or pause mode. We forget more often. It is important to keep purposes that are not related to our aging bodies, as well. Do not let your focus become too narrow. Without neglecting your body find goals that go beyond its maintenance.

Wholehearted effort is valuable in itself. Constructively directed wholehearted effort is even more worthwhile. When success falls into your hands without effort on your part the results can be harmful. As much as possible do your best in each moment. Then life is a gift partially earned.

Do you already know that you can't hold on to anything? Health will come and go; love, too; intellect, friends and relatives will leave in one way or another. Religious belief will merge and fade and merge and fade, sometimes forgotten. Even the precious routines and rituals you use to hold on to life will be disrupted and evolve. Life can't be preserved with paintings or photos or solid houses or dependable cars or secure jobs or careful monitoring of your health, or dutiful application of cosmetics. Watch everything change over time. So treasure the now. Reality has to keep finding new ways to support you, whether you realize it or not.

Monks in Japan were sent to graveyards to meditate and reflect on their future. These days I suggest you invest some time visiting and/or volunteering in nursing homes and hospitals. If you live long enough you will spend some of your future in such settings. Discover the good and the bad, the life and the death, the joy and the misery in such settings. Relish the possibilities in your now, wherever you live.

Slight annoyances and minor inconveniences and paltry slights and trivial preferences shift our lives away from doing what we know to be right. We may take a proper stand on a few notably big issues and contort ourselves on what we consider to be "minor" ones. Beware! Most of your life is spent on "small" tasks, moment by moment. Whatever character may be, it is built on the moment-by-moment attention to these "small" tasks. Even the relative security of good habits earned by thoughtful repetition holds no guarantee. Keep on refining yourself.

After a few dry, warm days in winter a sudden chill with light precipitation may make roads suddenly slick. It pays to travel particularly slowly and carefully under such conditions of life. While pondering the deeper meanings of what you read don't fail to greet others with a smile, hurry across crosswalks to save gasoline for waiting drivers and the earth, offer thanks to mail carriers and trash collectors and cashiers.

Like success and profit, failure and loss bring forth what needs to be done next. Gloating or berating or wallowing also elicit what needs to be done next. What else is there? No one escapes or rearranges this sequence of moments and arisings of what needs doing. Neither diligence nor neglect turns off the order. Respond responsibly.

There are no temptations out there, only the tempted. You choose how to fit yourself to the rest of Reality. Perspectives determine whether a software element is a bug or a feature. Similarly, perspectives determine temptations and opportunities. Your perspectives don't determine mine, and my perspectives don't determine yours. Nevertheless, we sometimes act as though they did.

We have neither time nor inclination to figure out all the ramifications of every behavior. On the whole aim to do little harm, much good, what you know to be right and exemplary and fitting to the circumstances that appear.

However impressive your public face, you know what lies behind it. Lies beget more lies. Truth beckons truth. Allow Reality to bake you through and through. Become flavorful.

It is easier to point out the sweet and sour in others than to evaluate the complexity of taste in yourself. Work on your own nutrition. You are not the expert gourmet for the world. Neither am I. So take my cookbooks with a grain of salt.

Life is lived moment by moment. Right or wrong is case by case. Waiting or going ahead is decided by circumstances. I offer you no static rules, even this one. Whatever needs doing emerges. Pay attention.

You can handle the riding of life's waves; you can handle the pounding of life's waves. Whether you actually do so or not is up to you. Your preparation for life was provided by your living. Use your life experience well. Not having lived anyone else's life we cannot know the preparations and circumstances of others. Yet we sometimes think we can.

Don't be fooled by dress or titles or money or fame or where a person lives. Monasteries don't necessarily make one religious or universities make one scholarly or psychotherapy make one mentally healthy or hospitals make one well. You know that. What, then, makes one worthy, trustworthy, praiseworthy, lifeworthy? The worthiness rests on what one does again and again, always new, reaching a personal standard of doing with some consistency.

Regardless of the fluctuations of fate, keep to your honorable course. Your successes are gifts from Reality, too, so don't puff yourself up with pride. Earn the chance of success with good effort.

The tales of history are myths, Reality pared down to fit in books and lectures. The complexities and confusions of everyday life don't get written in legends of princes and presidents. Don't aim to imitate the fancied exploits of these mythical historic figures. Be realistic. Comparing yourself to cartoon heroes of history is meaningless. Beware particularly the inflated images of religious and political figures. Imagine them sweating with upset stomachs and headaches.

It is good practice to begin each morning with attention to goals and purposes and appreciation of another opportunity to fulfill them. No one is guaranteed awakening from sleep. How kind of Reality to provide opportunity and support in our endeavors! Concrete, specific, doable goals allow us to gauge our accomplishments and failures more accurately than vague, abstract dreaming.

Similarly, it is good practice in the evening to reflect on what was accomplished, what assistance was received, what was given to others, and what troubles were caused others during that day. The mind naturally turns then to what needs to be accomplished the next day, what assistance is likely to be received, how others can be repaid, and how troubles and inconveniences to others can be reduced. Following these reflections it is time to lie down and submit the mind to the curtain of sleep.

Sometimes it is appropriate to put off what needs doing for a more suitable time. Circumstances may need ripening. Other, more immediate, action may be required. However, putting off necessary action because of sloth or fear or other intrusive feelings must be avoided. Behaviors repeated become habits. Habits form lifestyles. We become what we do. What we did defines what we did not do.

Situations keep changing. We must fit ourselves to the changing situations. Some circumstances require openness; some require secrecy. Some require aggressiveness; some require avoidance. Challenges can be invitations or traps. Seek more information when in doubt. It is often helpful to check the reliability of your information sources.

Many cultures have special days or situations in which some of the usual social rules are suspended. Be aware of those special circumstances and use them circumspectly. Do not knowingly cause harm to others even if you are guaranteed escape from punishment.

Watching television or listening to music all day trains your brain to ignore talk and music most of the time while you focus on housework or running or driving or eating or some other task. You quickly forget the content of television programs, sometimes watching the same one twice. Can training your brain to forget be a contributor to the increasing incidence of Alzheimer's disease? Be sure to schedule long periods of silence in your everyday life. In your room alone, walking along a mountain trail, while driving or waiting in line, create time for quiet reflection. If circumstances permit invest whole days in complete silence. Get acquainted with your mind. Learn its preferences and habits; watch the patterns of recurring thoughts; notice what you noticed and what you failed to notice. Embrace the range of your creativity, including obsessions and fears. Respond to what appears that needs doing.

Write more; talk less. Writing allows us to communicate more carefully and clearly. Words are too often thrown away thoughtlessly in speech, causing unnecessary trouble to others and self. When possible, slow your speech to writing pace. If you were here I would give the same advice.

I remain hidden not because of shyness, but to avoid distractions and pride. I did my share of public appearances in the past. Now is the time to quietly offer you information accumulated over more than seventy years. By now, I know what works for me whether I consistently implement it or not. We humans share a proclivity for experimentation.

Happiness, fun, and desires are all just fine, in their proper place. They are not the whole of life, just another subset of goals pulling action from us. Without them life would be grim and aimless. Satisfaction arrives when a purpose is discovered and effort is made to attain it. When purposes are successfully attained a particular kind of satisfaction appears, even though the results of our efforts might bring auxiliary consequences that are less pleasant. Asceticism is merely a matter of reducing goals to make them more attainable. One kind of satisfaction is enhanced at the expense of other kinds.

Recognize and accept your imperfection. Work on your debts to people and things. Gloomy self-abasement is selfish and unpleasant for others. Use your imperfection as well as you can. The person who needs your best advice most is yourself.

Wealth and power are maintained by careful suspicion and fear of losing them. The more you possess the more you aim to protect. To possess nothing at all causes trouble for others who must support your dependency. Find some middle ground so that you are not distracted from worthy pursuits. Earn enough to maintain your body's condition as well as possible. It is your body that gets your doing done.

You will have moments of exhaustion, pain, weakness, and disability. The body you thought you governed will seem to turn against you. While dealing with your misery realistically discover new goals and possibilities. Use these moments to expand your range of abilities. Nurture those who serve you and those who suffer alongside you. The minimal thanks and a smile are usually possible. While waiting for relief do what you can.

No matter what you believe about your importance, you are not the central focus in the eyes of others. For many you are little more than a means to their own ends. Yet you are surrounded by their services and gifts. You did not make all the parts of your computer or television or vehicle. You did not create all the ingredients in your food. You were not born an adult with knowledge of your language or your work. Unimportant and imperfect, we are blessed.

Social and psychological death comes when we stop learning. Notice and learn from your environment, including your body. Discover new ways to wash dishes, clean the shower, toilet, dress, dust, write, listen, walk, and other ways to do your life. Never become so satisfied with your life that you stop seeking ways to improve it. Whatever the results of your investigations and practices it is the searching and discovering that is vital.

Of course you prepare for retirement. However, no one retires from life at retirement age. Develop skills and interests that extend into your later years. Keep body and mind moving as much as health permits. Find new ways to give yourself away. Don't turn off living until you die. Aging will impress you with your need to submit yourself to Reality and your need to operate within realistic limits.

It is more important to remember than to be remembered. As your memory slips away and your attention is pulled increasingly to your body, keep putting forth your best efforts. Life never becomes purposeless; rather, purposes evolve. When finished reading put away your book or computer carefully, with attention. If remembered at all, we shall be remembered for what we did, the indirect and objective reflections of our thoughts and feelings.

As with any feeling you can distract yourself to avoid feeling guilt. Nevertheless, guilt carries information that must be acknowledged. What needs to be done in this matter? There is nothing wrong with pleasure; there is nothing wrong with the feelings (pleasant and unpleasant) that well up in your mind. So unnecessary guilt is just fine, too. Appreciate its meaning and move on with constructive activity.

Those around you may or may not acknowledge your wisdom, your good effort, your service, your contributions to mankind, and your gifts to the earth. Recognized or not, keep on doing what you know is right. If not a model for others, at least be a model for yourself. You know what you do in private.

If life always went smoothly, how little prepared we would be for a moment of trouble. Use life's difficult moments to build patience and perseverance. When the obvious rewards of recognition and wealth fail to appear, you can more clearly see other goals that call to you. You know what needs to be done, what you were born to do...however the results turn out.

You know best what is hardest for you to do. You know best what distracts you from what really needs doing. You know best the tactics you use to delay important purposeful activity. Search for new and useful ways to keep yourself on track, carrying out the realistic tasks that beckon you.

Learn from the mistakes of others and from their successes, too. Such lessons are personally less expensive yet potentially quite valuable. You will miss many of these lessons if you aren't paying attention. How kind of others (including parents) to provide us with examples of what to do and what not to do! Yet it is you who defines your life. Actions become habits, and habits format your character. Life lessons are of no value unless applied diligently again and again.

It is our nature to look out for ourselves. Redefining the self to include a wider range of phenomena allows us to transcend our narrow self-interest. Dissolving the self in Reality, in situations and circumstances, allows us to find new satisfaction in service and sacrifice. In fact, even the words "service" and "sacrifice" lose their meaning. What decides what needs doing?

Look for peaceful solutions, for innovative kindness, for soft words, for creative gifts, for clear truth. Make it easy for others to interpret your acts as helpful and good. Minimize complaints and excuses. Accept what comes your way and use it constructively. Aim for simplicity when possible because complexity makes constructive purposes harder to determine. Of course, sometimes complexity cannot be avoided. Accept complexity, too.

Gossip and criticism of others serves to distract us from our own faults and limitations. A careful examination reveals innumerable troubles we cause to others and a panoply of gifts and services we receive from them. Find honest ways to praise and thank your enemies.

When you have done something that is good and right and properly fitting your situation then you will feel a satisfaction that no one can take away from you. Material wealth and public attention are fragile in the sense that they are always subject to others' actions and interests. Knowing that you have done what constructively needed doing is truly yours. Others can see your behavior and guess at your intent, but you know what you were about whatever results may appear. All results simply present another set of circumstances for subsequent constructive doing. How kind of Reality to keep presenting us with opportunities for right action!

Can you imagine yourself without your family, friends, workplace, living space, your senses, your memories, and your body? It is the boundaries that shape and define us. We carve ourselves out of Reality. There is nothing else. At any given moment the quality of your actions place you on the dimensional range from loving kindness to dutiful responsibility. More boundaries. Shaping us as Reality (and we) keep appearing and changing.

To advise you to stop comparing yourself with others would be foolish. We humans compare. The frivolous and shallow comparisons that we customarily make often lead to unnecessary suffering. I recommend finer, more realistic, comparisons. Watch the ongoing changes in others; look for details; learn from them. Comparisons are quite useful when properly employed.

The longer we live the more we learn of the deaths of friends, relatives, lovers and others familiar and unfamiliar to us. Like all feelings grief fades over time unless restimulated. These deaths remind us that life is limited, connections are impermanent, deeds must be done while we live, and others will someday face our own deaths. These reminders fade over time, too. The best preparation for death is to live well the days Reality allows you.

Sometimes we think we deserve better than what comes our way. Less often we think we deserve

less. That anything at all appears with its challenging invitations to do what needs doing is often an

unrecognized gift. Who remains ever worthy of such largesse?

From the outside some kinds of play look like hard work, requiring lots of time and effort. From

the inside some kinds of work are filled with fun, like play. So work and play are not pure

opposites. They both oppose sloth, boredom, and lack of constructive purpose. Enjoyment is about

constructive, purposeful activity. Depth is about recognizing how much of one's constructive,

purposeful activity is thanks to others. Prideful, haughty behavior elicits envy and enemies.

Humble behavior is simply realistic and truthful.

When all seems to be going well, there is no way to preserve the status quo. People die, machines

break down, houses need repairs, weeds grow, insects attack, tempers flare, the body rebels,

economic markets drop, sources dry up, memory fails, and other changes occur to undermine

periods of relative tranquility. We do what we can to prepare for and forestall tragedies and

inconveniences, but there is no way to eliminate them. The sensible response is to respond

realistically to them. What needs doing next? As you already know, it is one thing to understand

this principle intellectually and quite another thing to carry it out consistently.

You can expect to have moments of self-criticism and mild depression. Such moments are not

illness even though they may be temporarily masked by medication. While feeling sad and

doubtful turn to what needs doing next. Move your body in constructive directions. Find ways to

be helpful and useful to others. Prove to yourself that feelings need not dominate and govern your

life. Responding to these challenges repeatedly you learn one of life's most valuable lessons. Did you think that those you most respect and honor don't face moments of misery, self-criticism, and despair? What you see is what they did and do, not what they felt.

The more skillful you become at life, the more details you see. The more details you see, the better you can refine your life. There is no end to constructive tweaking. The alternative is unused potential and random, unnecessary suffering. One way or another, our brains are on the move. Keep on putting your imagination to work; you need not try to shut it down. Find meaning in your misery. Turn tragedy into the precursor of positive action. For what else were you presented with these precious life moments?

You have eyes to see with, ears to hear with, and so on. Do not let your senses go to waste by excessive rumination. Going over and over what happened in the past or rehearsing future possibilities again and again distracts you from the ever-changing world your senses can inform you about. Besides being boring ruts don't allow you to respond realistically to what presents itself to you.

How is it that these words make sense to us? It is not a matter merely of understanding the meaning of each word and phrase. The point of the underlying message pokes through at times. The gestalt surprises me, too, as I write and reread. I become astonished by the wholeness of it. Perhaps the same interpreter of what needs to be done also explains the gist of this writing...at least to those who really want to understand.

To imagine that I am special, talented, wise, deep, kind, and insightful is to miss the point of momentary gifts received and to set myself up for disappointment in the moments when I am stupid, forgetful, unkind, and so forth. I make ordinary mistakes and have ordinary misunderstandings. Despite being ordinary, I see extraordinary largesse coming to this undeserving human. Don't mistake these words for frontal humility. Reality deserves praise, not me. Gurus must put on a show. I don't. A few days ago the laundry room floor was covered in water. The day before yesterday I injured my foot playing tennis. A fungus has attacked my fruit trees. These are merely more ordinary events requiring my response. There is no end to them until there is an end to them. Whoever offers you a smooth, trouble-free, peaceful life because you have special abilities that need developing is seeking something you possess. Don't be fooled.

Whether we understand the order or not Reality operates in an orderly fashion. That is not to say that Reality operates toward me in a consistently positive or negative fashion, as seen from my perspective. The order, the regularity, often goes unseen, interpreted through our self-centered lenses. We don't care much about gravitational forces as such while our plane hurtles toward the earth. While science continues to search for and discover this order, we most often view Reality in terms of our own convenience. The radio doesn't always play our favorite songs.

Love is a wonderful feeling, but it channels the vision and may result in irrational behavior. When love becomes the sole determinant of purposeful behavior we are likely to find ourselves in trouble. Enjoy the feeling, but keep alert. All feelings fade over time unless restimulated. However, the results of our actions may remain for years. Such advice is unlikely to be heard when we are in the throes of love.

Shared family membership does not insure shared values, shared caring, or even shared genes. Debts are accumulated within families, however, and should be repaid diligently. The general principles involving consideration of what was received from others, what was given to others, and the troubles caused others apply to family members as well. Focusing on the troubles others caused you is a self-serving way of avoiding consideration of the troubles you caused them and what you received from them. For example, when you were an infant someone fed you and washed you and changed your diapers whether they felt like it or not, whether you noticed it or not, whether you showed appreciation or not.

Enjoy the good feelings, too, and learn from them. However, have no illusions that they will last forever. No matter how you attempt to restimulate them, to keep them going, there will be times when the feelings you like will be gone. The worth of your life is not determined by what percentage of it is filled with happiness. Don't try to build your life on the shifting foundation of feelings. Such foolishness offers no long-term payoff to you or to those around you.

Neither is life built upon prosperity. There are obvious advantages to prosperity, but there are characteristic dangers, too. When riches lead to laziness, to haughtiness, to hiring others to do what the wealthy need to do, to paranoid protection of wealth, to unconcern with surrounding poverty, to maintaining appearances at the expense of truth, then riches become a burden.

Reality kindly presents me to me. I am valuable because I am one of Reality's representatives (a child of Reality, if you like), an aspect of Reality. This self worth hasn't been earned despite my efforts to maintain a positive self-image. My efforts to behave myself into feelings of self-esteem are useful in affecting how I view myself, but my underlying value as a part of Reality remains unaffected. So there is a distinction between absolute self worth and perceived self worth. "Hitting bottom" means giving up on the perceived self worth and encountering the reality that allows bouncing back. In religious circles the phrase "Let go and let God" is somewhat the same thing.

Doing good with kind, helpful behavior is an end in itself, but often the doing is accompanied by a bonus of good feelings. There is a built-in feeling reward for good behavior. That feeling is not merely an increase in self-esteem. Self-monitoring may even disappear while doing good. The recipient or the doing itself may take full screen. Only doing good permits this particular set of good feelings.

Love is wandering around lost outside of you with no desire for a map to get home. Love prompts us to serve the other at all cost. In moments when we are wrapped up in ourselves we do not love, we calculate. Sometimes we can generate love by lots of dedicated service. Serving enemies is the most effective way to turn them into lovable friends. Conquering enemies generates neither love nor friends, but more self-interested calculations.

Suffering doesn't necessarily produce endurance, but it helps. Every tragedy kindly presents the opportunity to respond in a positive way. Thus we have the chance to develop a wider repertoire of positive behaviors to a wider range of situations. Suffering happens; what we do about it is up to us.

Holiness is in the eye of the beholder. Beware those who make efforts to appear holy. There is nothing holier than the Reality that surrounds you, is you. The payoff for fancy titles and colored robes and elegant buildings and religious talk and mystical chanting is here on earth, make no mistake about it. Faith in supernatural powers is optional. Religious faith can help dissolve self-centeredness, but not always. Beware anyone who promotes faith as a means to make you feel special.

Develop a skill using your hands as well as your mind. Paint or fix motorcycles or build sheds or garden or quilt or find another way to produce some tangible, immediate product of your labor. The modern world too often works to spirit us away from the concrete reality that is before our eyes. We no longer understand how things work, how to fix them when they break down. We replace whole appliances or appliance parts or we call professionals to do so. There is benefit in having some hands-on skills. We become more practically embedded in situations as we physically interact with them. There are limits to virtual reality schemes and theoretical constructions. The tears on your television screen are not real tears.

Our lives are full of might-have-beens had we done something differently. There are endless possibilities of occurrences and situations that never happened. What we do interacts with circumstances and produces, sometimes, unanticipated results. In this vast array of possibility we are fortunate that moments appear to us one at a time. The problem is not "What shall I do in all possible situations at all times?" but "What shall I do here and now?" Given that we do not recognize and understand all that is going on in a single moment, nevertheless we respond with what we do perceive. Then, of course, the results are no more than what appears for us in the next moment, inviting our next response.

It isn't unusual to encounter at least a few people who don't like you. You have no responsibility to be likeable to everyone. Individuals have individual tastes. Allow others to have their own preferences. The simplest solution to dealing with those who dislike you is to avoid them when possible. When circumstances require you to interact with them recall the kindnesses you have received from them and let them know that you remember their acts of generosity and service to you. Apologize for the troubles and inconveniences you have caused them. Continue to hold to your own purposes; you need not be pushed around as a result of your words. You may discover that your openness turns enemies into friends. Or you may not. In either case, you have presented a model that may surprise and invite imitation.

Preparing for suffering and preparing for joy are both part of a sound life plan. A solid foundation for dealing with suffering requires some objectivity. Keep attuned to the specific ways in which Reality supports you. Even when miserable that support continues--the air flows into your lungs, your body processes food, your senses provide you with fresh information, and new moments keep appearing. When you find yourself troubled, feeling gratitude or not, maintain some realistic perspective. Build a history of maintaining equilibrium through suffering so you can recall how you made it through past troubles with some success. Remember that feelings fade over time unless restimulated. Remember that feelings will fade when joy presents itself, too. Enjoy the moment, but don't try to build your life on feeling good all the time. Life becomes more stable as you develop skills at doing what needs doing while noting feelings but not letting them be the sole determinants of what you do.

Obey the laws when you deem them to be just and without harm to others. Be willing to bear the consequences when you break the law, apprehended or not. Many laws are created by persons in power for the benefit of persons in power. Whether you are in power or not it is sensible to know laws that affect you and use them wisely. Laws are not absolute; they change. We change, too, and so does our use of laws.

Orderliness helps us find things when we need them. Keeping things in their place and weeding out outdated papers may be chores, but one benefit appears when we search for something. When a room is clean and neat, intentionally placing an object out of its place presents an obvious visible reminder of something that needs doing. Such a useful clue isn't meaningful when the space is untidy. Clearing out items that are no longer useful gives opportunity to reexamine one's past and prepare donations.

Humans compare themselves with others. We notice the clothing they wear, their successes and failures, their looks, their health, their skills, and so forth. Comparing is natural, but building self-praise or self-scolding on the basis of comparisons is unnecessary. Even while comparing yourself with the yourself of the past, avoid tying your mind up in rumination. Your life is being built on what you do now. Do it well. That doing is exactly good enough.

Anyone who takes the time to check it out realizes that happiness, fame, insight, youth, and perfect health don't last forever. A variety of changes keeps presenting itself to us. Shinky (oversensitive) people get worried about how long the good times and good feelings will last. The sensible course is to recognize the inevitability of change and dance with it. I see nothing wrong with doing what we can to extend the good times as long as we keep in mind that preserving them as they are is hopeless. Enjoying the downturns is possible, too. The whole tableau is, well, interesting.

Thoughts can be helpful or troublesome. Obsessive thoughts are reminders that you once thought something important. Trying to stop thinking about something directly usually increases the likelihood of thinking the undesired thoughts. Thank your mind for its imaginativeness and turn your body to some absorbing, and constructive, activity. Constructive activity is likely to be helpful in redirecting attention away from troublesome thoughts. Even if the rumination continues some constructive goal is accomplished. Much of the problem with obsessive thinking comes from the idea that such thoughts are the only thing of importance in life, that there is no real life until those thoughts are vanquished. Put those thoughts in their proper place by continuing with a positive, goal-directed, purposeful set of behaviors.

You can fool some of the people all of the time, but you can't fool Reality. You can fool all of the people (including yourself) some of the time, but you can't fool the larger Reality. What is, is. The honest, straightforward, clear perspective has realistic payoff.

Everyone wants to be loved, respected, and treasured. However, there is no way of forcing others to love, respect, and treasure us. Behaving lovingly and respectfully toward others is controllable, even though sometimes difficult. You can't get rid of your desires, but you can monitor them to see that they don't interfere with your doing what needs to be done. For example, in your desire for love, don't give up your life goals, and don't set hurtful goals toward others. Considering the way Reality keeps supporting you, couldn't you consider that being loved?

When time permits, delay your major decision awhile. Especially when your action is connected with a strong feeling, give your mind time to make a rational, realistic decision. Avoid making enemies unnecessarily; when possible, choose a course that supports and encourages others.

Take time to eat slowly, with attention, small portions of food on small plates and bowls. The rewards of less weight and longer life are supplemented by appreciation of the taste and the effort that went into food preparation. My body responds to light exercise after a meal, and gentle twisting of the torso and stretching. Experiment to find out what works for your body after eating.

To know all about Constructive Living without practicing it in everyday life is not to know it at all. To be merely a scholar of Constructive Living is to miss the point of it. Let the principles seep into your body until you are immersed in Realistic thought and action. At least borrow what is useful.

Grabbing all you can for yourself is a game you cannot win. There is always more to take, always more to protect. Giving yourself away to others is a game you can win because there is always more of you to give away, always more who are in need of your giving.

Because feelings and thoughts keep fluctuating some sort of focus is necessary to lead a useful and productive life. You can choose the particular focus that you find most fitting. I have suggested attending to each moment's message about what Reality is sending to do. An overall focus helps you sort out the variety of stimuli that appear to you, honing in on the relevant information related to what needs doing. Don't let waves of feelings and thoughts toss you about haphazardly. Construct habits of realistic action centered on your focus. Reflect on your focus now and then to make sure it is current.

Sometimes what needs doing is to rest. Resting may involve napping or sitting on a bench between games or moving to a different sort of task or something else. Think of rest as both an end in itself and as a means to recharge yourself for the next things that need doing. Feeling guilt about resting is just another feeling. If there is too much rest, interfering with vital tasks, then guilt contains information that needs action. Rest and work are realistic elements of an enjoyable life.

Feeling humiliated is possible only where there is pride. Humiliation has its essence in contrast. Recognizing the multitude of specific ways in which we are supported by Reality helps reduce the likelihood of feeling humiliated. Something keeps taking care of us even when our pride is damaged.

Attempts to please everyone all the time are doomed to failure. Attempts to save others from their destructive lifestyles are also fruitless. You can offer advice and support, but individuals must save themselves or not at all. Choose your purposes carefully. Choose purposes that are realistic, with specific outcomes that have the possibility of coming about. Review immediate and long-term purposes often. You will die someday. Do not forget this inevitability when selecting purposes.

Get lost...in your circumstances. Use attention and purposes to guide you. Your trail through the jungle of stimuli has been blazed for you by the Reality of people and other creatures and things and a variety of phenomena visible and invisible. You may not be able to see the trail far ahead, but looking back it becomes apparent. The clearings here and there may surprise you, but the end of the trail is certain. Make your trail a model for other hikers.

You do not need medication to solve every single problem that appears in your life. Actual physical illnesses may require medicine, but beware the appeal by some interests to define any difficulty a medical problem. Even if drugs could make it easier to shop less, pay your bills regularly, eat less and exercise more, take fewer chances, even smile more, you pay the price of giving up areas of your life to chemical control. The more you take responsibility for your own behavior, the more you exert the control you have over your own behavior, the freer you are. There is a natural tension between freedom and comfort.

Sometimes we cause trouble and inconvenience to others. Our very existence is a burden to them at times--for example, when drivers must wait for us to cross the street at a crosswalk. Whether or not you feel remorse and guilt upon recognizing the trouble you cause others in a particular situation is not controllable. However, you should be aware of these troubles and apologize when appropriate. I even apologize to my computer and toaster and microwave oven when I make them wait. I thank my car for starting up promptly, too. These courtesies are reminders to me of their role in making my life easier and productive. Whether filled with gratitude or not, I am acknowledging reality.

Plans and outcomes don't always progress at the pace we desire or expect. Sometimes too fast, sometimes too slow, events occur at their own pace. In any case, they bring the messages of what needs to be done. Learn to be a good observer of unfolding events. Watch yourself unfold as part of them.

Respect and admiration for another person may be caused by your ignorance about the details of their everyday behavior. You know most about yourself. You have the opportunity to make yourself into a truly admirable person. We all depend on others for our existence.

Overdependency is just laziness. Select friends and business associates you can trust. Be the sort of person others can trust because you are realistic. Don't let friendship or companionship interfere with more important purposes. It is better to be alone and purposeful than to submit to the random tides of a group.

Words are very rough approximations of reality, even these words. Recognize the difference between "fish" and a fish and that wriggling creature over there. Your actions are real, whatever you call them, whatever value you place on them, however you conceive them. Build your life, your life history, on constructive, purposeful action.

If you keep peeling back the sources of our knowledge, you encounter a mystery. How do we know what we think we know? Where do our ideas about what we think we know come from? Knowledge is not really a thing, like a book or a candle. Some knowledge seems to be expressed in words, but other forms include an overhead smash in tennis and the flick of the wrist in fly-fishing and the steering of an automobile. In a sense, knowledge happens to us. We may do something to encourage it, such as study and practice, but there are no guarantees that our actions will consistently produce the desired knowledge. In the end it is a mysterious gift. As you grow older you will understand this point better; that understanding, too, is a gift of knowledge.

What other people think and say about you is their concern. You can influence your public image, but you cannot control it. Your behavior, however honest and straightforward, is open to interpretation by others. Construct your life on your own values and not on the image in others' eyes. Your judgment of what you need to do is paramount. Be prepared to bear the punishment for your actions if the judgment of others considers you worthy of it. Know the rules by which others judge.

Reality responds to our actions. If the response repeatedly brings pain and loss and other forms of misery, then our behavior needs reexamination. What needs to be done differently? Rather than considering stopping a behavior, it is more fruitful to consider substituting another behavior for the behavior that isn't working well. Wanting to change the behavior, deciding to change the behavior, resolving to change the behavior, choosing to change the behavior--all these mental steps are unnecessary. Just change the doing itself. However difficult, the course is simple and straightforward.

You are always doing something, even when waiting. You may be sitting, staring at a computer screen while waiting for a file to download. You may be lying in bed waiting for sleep to come. There are a variety of bodily activities and mental exercises you can employ to make the waiting time more interesting, enjoyable, and constructive. The time you live through while waiting will not be returned to you. Keep handy the lists, puzzles, reading material, writing material, flash cards, music instruments, and other physical and mental gear that allow you to use your time well while waiting.

Strange as it may seem, the best way to recover from post traumatic stress disorder is to do good to others. Finding someone in need and doing our best to help them moves attention away from the suffering self and serves as a reminder that we are not alone in suffering. It is rather common to believe that our misery is special, unique, and beyond the understanding of others. Working to relieve the unnecessary misery around us puts our suffering in perspective and adds meaning to it.

There are many social rewards for looking good to others. In many respects the easiest way to appear upright is to actually behave in an upright manner. Then there is no wasted effort covering up hidden deceits and faults. However, humans that we are, the course of constant purity is exceedingly difficult. In fact, our very existence causes all sorts of troubles to others whether we realize it or not. We create waste; we consume resources others might use; we occupy positions and hold wealth others might benefit from were we not there; we cause others to wait; we put others in positions where they are rewarded for lying and pilfering; and so forth. Imperfect though we are, Reality keeps taking care of us. Nevertheless, the social rewards for looking good should not be ignored.

Moments of sadness, grief, and despair are normal. In those moments we forget the overwhelming support that Reality keeps generously offering us. Whether or not we notice the largesse or feel thankful for it in those moments, it keeps presenting itself to us. Complaining to anyone, including a psychotherapist, is not therapeutic. It merely shows a lack of awareness.

We somehow know what is right to do; we somehow know what needs to be done. No one really knows how. Sometimes we do what needs doing; sometimes we don't. No one knows why. There are many stories about the causes of our knowledge and actions. Some of the stories are complicated and academic. Some of the stories are like folk tales, easily dismissed. Whatever the true causes, you know what you know and you do what you do. You are responsible for the actions that lie within your physical capabilities. Those actions define you as a good or bad person in any given moment. They hold the key to moral trustworthiness and realistic responses to circumstances. And we all make up stories about the why of them. Maintain a measure of doubt about those stories.

When asked for counseling or advice, offer it. Base your offering on your own experience, not on something you read in a book or on a computer screen. Do not require your advice to be followed, however. You are not permitted to decide what others need to do. Others may use the information you provided in ways you did not even imagine. The good news is that you are not responsible for what they do either.

Even though we lack access to the totality of information about people we rate them anyway. Our judgments about them are biased and may be hard to change. Nevertheless, our estimates of others affect how we interact with them. Giving to others what we think they need is not the same as giving them what we think they think they want.

Our imaginations of heavenly perfection are projected extensions of ordinary good. Tacking on "extremely" doesn't really change the quality of a momentary mind.

Our lack of knowledge is unbounded, even by our modesty. I don't know how little I know. What I do know is borrowed temporarily. What I thought I did know so often turns out to be wrong. Always somewhat out of date, I keep on updating myself. My expertise is fluid. How little I knew back then...and now. The gaps don't prevent me from acting, however. Knowing better, forgetting mostly, I trust the fluid, pretending it is rock hard. Do you see these petroglyphs flowing before your eyes?

I'm not dead yet as I write these words. You probably figured that out, even if I hadn't pointed it out. It is thanks to a lot of careful drivers and medical support and borrowed genes and food produced by strangers in various countries and trained pilots and so on that I still live. I do my part with exercise and nutrition and minimizing risks and the like, but so much could go wrong in spite of my efforts. We can talk about odds and statistics, but hidden within those numbers is the single case of me--the case that makes a great difference to me no matter what the generalities tell us. I know that almost all of the people whose efforts keep me alive have never heard of me. Nevertheless, the whole complex system works as though it were set up to sustain my life. Yours, too. Recognize and acknowledge it or not, it works for me. And you.

Rest is wonderful after hours of exertion hiking in the mountains or cleaning house or weeding the garden. Rest is wonderful when earned. Rest can be boring when nothing much precedes it. It can be a time filler, an escape from some necessary activity, a way to avoid someone or something, an excuse, an alibi. Rest may involve lying down or shifting to another task for a reviving change of pace. Appreciate the opportunity and the sources making rest possible.

Evaluate the truth of these words with your own experience. Don't simply base your beliefs on someone else's expertise. If you don't recognize yourself in my writing then perhaps you should examine other mirrors. I write what makes sense to me. What else can I do honorably? How kind of you to welcome me into your thoughts. Let your actions determine the worth of these principles of living. I did not build this ark, I only present my perspective on its blueprints. How fortunate that it appears to be reasonably constructed. I'll continue to verify its sturdiness and point out its details. That is what I am in the world to do.

Some days don't go well. They stand out because most days do. Expectations of the ordinary are typical. The unexpected, the unusual gets our attention. Use the unexpected as a tool for learning, not as an excuse for complaining. Whatever appears prompts "What needs doing now?" How kind of Reality to toss lessons at us. Do you catch on?

How to live a life of maximum service to others and minimum troubles to others is quite complicated when you think below the surface. You decide what is a service and what is a trouble. Your definitions of services and troubles have been influenced by the definitions of others around you. Your definitions are, at least in part, borrowed. Your service to others is with borrowed energy, a borrowed body, and borrowed definitions. So give thanks as you serve. Both giving and receiving deserve thanks. There is no way we can earn the largesse we receive, no way we can give enough to deserve it. Whatever continues to ignite those moment-to-moment ongoing flashes of life permits us the privilege of serving others.

What can you give when you are very old or very ill? When your body and resources are limited, what can you offer to others? Humor, information, compliments, smiles, and thanks are among the gifts you can give even under conditions of scarcity. Don't underestimate the value of such gifts.

You prepare for life by living it. You can't step outside of life in order to pull yourself together. There is no alternative to dealing with Reality other than dealing with Reality. For all your hopes and dreams and forecasts Reality comes to you as it comes. Do your life well.

Rational, idealistic deliberations are fine, but find ways to actualize them. Unless implemented, such mental exercises are like mountain fog--dissipating, reemerging, fading, reappearing.

We all have secrets. We haven't time to tell everything about us, and others have no time to listen to all of it. Some secrets, however, need to be exposed. By revealing them and dedicating ourselves to full disclosure in that area we admit others more fully into our lives. Reveal the secrets that others need to hear, not necessarily the ones you need to get out in the open. The act of self-exposure is for the convenience of others, not for our own convenience. What is best for them to know?

Who are your children? Who are your brothers and sisters? Who are your ancestors? If you think only in terms of blood-related kin your view is too narrow. You are surrounded by people and things who deserve kinship.

As I hike in the mountains of Japan I must ask directions of strangers. They smile and kindly send me off in the right direction. They appear happy to be helpful to this foreigner. All they get in return is a smile and thanks. We take pleasure in being able to give even a small something to others--a greeting, information, a smile, a few kind words. Recognize the occasion when it arises.

Criticism provokes a desire to respond. Responses may be defensive or attacking or informative or supportive or no response at all. You must decide whether a response and what sort of response needs to be done. Keep in mind that your response may elicit further responses from the person who originated the criticism. I find myself these days often either thanking the person for their input and getting on to other matters or offering no response at all. What can I offer in return to someone who went to the trouble to evaluate me or my work?

I suspect that many people watch television crime dramas in order to view worlds in which order and justice ultimately prevail. In the real world of many changes it is reassuring to confirm a perspective of stability and confirmed expectations. Real life doesn't always turn out as we expect or deserve. Enjoy your fantasies of designated orderliness, but be flexible in response to what actually appears for you.

How much detail of my life I have forgotten! How many paths I have shortened in memory! The obvious pros and cons of such a tendency are apparent. Nevertheless, I wonder about important losses due to the templates of memory. What rules for forgetting have changed over these seventy-plus years? Writing doesn't really "preserve" anything. Each time I reread my earlier writing I see it with new eyes. But, then, remembering is no different. The past is gone forever.

Yoshimoto Ishin said that there is no way to repay God. Thomas A. Kempis wrote the same thing in The Imitation of Christ. Some debts can never be repaid. Yet we are obliged to try. I owe you, too, even though we may never have met. This writing is the best I can offer you right now.

Losing myself in writing or playing tennis or reading or some other project is a relief from self-consciousness. Usually, my mind skitters around that self-center until it finds something worthwhile to dive into. When lost in some activity rather than directing my thoughts, the thoughts simply well up as needed. They happen, and it would even be a mistake to write that they happen to me. Afterwards, on reflection, I can claim them. But not at the time they appear.

As curious as I am, as committed to knowing and understanding, there are endless mysteries I shall never fathom. Nevertheless, until convinced otherwise, I'll trust my interpreted experience of reality as truth.

COMMENTS ON THE ZEN TEACHINGS OF MAZU

I use as a source here Thomas Cleary's translation of The Zen Teachings of Mazu. Mazu Daoyi (709–788) was a famous Chan (Zen) master in China during the Tang Dynasty. His unique character and style of teaching are recorded in a variety of famous Buddhist works of that period.

Let's be reasonable. You can't reject your mind with your mind. That effort would involve rejecting the rejection and so on endlessly. You can't turn off subjective judgments. You can't eliminate desires. Your pleasures give you both joy and sorrow. At the very least they don't last at the same intensity forever. Suffering happens, but so does joy.

Attempting to do the impossible is, by definition, bound to fail to achieve the desired results. Aiming to force the mind to eliminate desires or feelings or judgments is not only a waste of time and energy. Aiming to force the mind leads to obsessions and increased misery. It is the aim of forcing that is the real problem. Accepting the reality of desires, feelings, and judgments is the most sensible course. They happen, okay, but they need not determine what you do. Thinking about dying is not dying. Thinking about overcoming anxiety is not overcoming anxiety. Deciding to do what is right is not doing what is right. Committing yourself to a course is not walking that course.

Thoughts, too, happen. By having in mind a purpose or goal some thoughts will flow in that direction. Whether the goal is quiet sitting or carving a pumpkin or writing a novel or sweeping the porch the purposeful activity helps direct thinking. Of course, stray thoughts will occur, too. Trying to suppress stray thoughts with the mind is useless and may stimulate even more thoughts unrelated to your goal. Returning your body to moving toward your goal is often helpful in reducing the distraction of stray thoughts.

Enlightened awareness of delusions does not free you from delusions. It may help free you of some of the power your customary thinking has over you. It may make you aware of ways to use your body, your actions, more realistically. It may help you have more moments noticing what is going on around/within you. Don't get the idea that some experience, however moving, will make your life endlessly clear of suffering and confusion. You may learn to accept being ordinary, nothing special.

The thing you call "a car" is not a car. The things you call "suffering" and "neurosis" and "hunger" and "desires" are not the things themselves. Furthermore, they are not "things" at all. Labels point at other labels. Your "mind" is "labeled." I'm merely stringing labels here to "explain" more labels. Is it possible to step back from this labeling and perceive reality in its raw form? I don't know. I don't care. It is enough for me to recognize the tendency to label, to organize and store information in labeled format. This recognition offers me a new (meta) set of labels with somewhat more "freedom to act", whatever that may be.

Reality keeps appearing to itself, never failing. Whether or not the current version appeals to us, it continues to show up. Whatever imprint our actions make on it, there it is again. However we interpret it, make sense of it, appeal to it, recognize it, meditate about it, or deny it, reality keeps emerging. It is no "it" except as we speak about it.

So delete unnecessary files, take out the trash, eat your meals, dress appropriately, answer the door, and so forth. Grasp what can be grasped, and do what is necessary and right. Do your best in the immersion. Now reading, now writing. Just be ordinary.

You never really know how much you don't know. You can't really grasp at once all that you do know. It is enough to know what you know now and what needs doing now.

Religions offer distinctive ways of talking about what is. They offer religious interpretations and meaning to what is. What is grows by incorporating them. So they end up talking about themselves.

If verbal explanations of verbal packages are satisfying to you then go ahead and play in that sandbox. Build castles and demolish them. Don't neglect to eat and bathe and exercise and sleep, however. You are sand of a sort.

Scholars and priests and judges and politicians are paid to offer sensible utterances. Sometimes useful, sometimes not, talk can never offer absolutely accurate depictions of reality. This talk, too. Nevertheless, you read and I write. Watch what people do.

Notice yourself feel eager or helpless or confident or joyful or perplexed or whatever. Notice yourself noticing yourself. Just like your feelings, your noticing is a gift. And so is your noticing your noticing. Accept the feelings and the noticing. Meanwhile, do what needs to be done. The doing is a gift, too. Relish your gifts. Relishing is a gift, too. In fact, you are just Reality's gift to you.

Everyone dies. Until you die your actions define your life. No one else feels what you feel or thinks what you think. Your actions, however, have direct effect on the lives around you. Your actions are your chance for repayment of Reality's gift.

REFLECTIONS ON THE ZAZEN YOJINKI

The Zazen Yojinki was written by Keizan Jokin Zenji (1268-1325). It has been translated by Yasuda Joshu Dainen roshi and Anzan Hoshin roshi (excerpted from the Treasury of Luminosity, also published in "The Art of Just Sitting: Essential Writings on the Zen Practice of Shikantaza" second edition, edited by John Daido Loori roshi, Wisdom Publications, 2004.

1

Consider carefully what is not, including the considering.

Recognize your tendencies, but do not let them lead you. They will cease to be tendencies in time.

The background from which all emerges is itself empty. There is no way to grasp it, no way to describe it, including "empty".

You see only what it reveals of itself, and not all of that. You never know what you missed. Even later.

The wider your perspective the less limited you are by others and by yourself.

Where is your mind? It is not in your brain. Sometimes it wanders, goes away, shrinks. It faces inward and outward and "noward". It isn't even yours.

You can't paste a reasonable label on its formlessness.

Images come floating in, like these words wrapped in associations. Happening.

Screen and images are not separate. The show starts right now.

2

While viewing the show, view the viewer viewing. Avoid becoming obsessed with the show, all the while appreciating it.

Feelings, too, are characters in the show, but they are no more main characters than other images. Don't let them take over the performance.

3

I don't know about a mind without thoughts or a body without movement. I do know about a mind not pushed around by emotions and a body that is at ease when that is one's purpose. One needs to keep checking on what the mind and body are about, including checking on the checking. It is not that mind and body are up to no good. Rather there are habits and routines that need to be explored and assisted, refined, or discarded. The measure is Reality. Fit yourself to Reality; merge yourself with Reality; immerse yourself as Reality.

4

Don't become obsessed with any activity. Maintain a flexible mind so you can see around corners and over hills and beyond precipices. Obsession with purposes is equally narrowing. Don't miss the angles. Search the perspectives of living creatures and all things. How is your keyboard doing today? Offer a smile and nod to your monitor.

Riches seduce one into maintaining them. Poverty incurs extraordinary assistance from others. Use well what you have, thoughtfully. Recognize gifts that appear without labels. Repairs are communications of thanks. Eating involves both gifts and repairs. Be reasonable.

5

Don't sit still for long periods. Move your body around. Walk for at least an hour or two a day when possible. Body movement helps you fight sleepiness when you want to stay awake and alert. Keep your head and face warm when it is cold, especially when you sleep. A towel across the forehead and eyes and bridge of the nose when in bed is a good idea if you have sinus problems. Breathe through the nose as much as possible.

Appreciate your imagination, your creative mind, but don't let it rule you. Odd thoughts are fine; they will pass away. Keep noticing what is going on around you. Good health allows for many options, but illness, too, is a teacher. If students come for teaching, teach; but don't go advertising for them. Students are our teachers, too. Trees instruct us also, so spend some time alone in natural surroundings. Mountains don't care who you are. Teaching doesn't make you wise or important or valuable. It is just something else that needs to be done sometimes.

You get no extra credit for unnecessarily causing yourself discomfort. You get no extra credit for living a life of luxury either. Use your resources with attention without wasting them. There is so much we don't know; it is foolish to be arrogant about what we do know.

Your body/mind responds to regular cleansing. So do those around you; don't offend them with filth and odors. Clean speech is part of good hygiene.

6

Your effort will vary from time to time. Your understanding and attention will vary from time to time. Your accomplishments will vary from time to time. Don't expect to sail your life in the sky on a permanent basis. Just do your educated best again and again. Doing so not only molds your life; it also provides a model for others. What causes you to have moments of clear, purposeful behavior no one knows. Accept the gifts as they appear. A variety of discoveries await you. Wisdom accumulates with experience, although it is not earned. Such wisdom is not Constructive Living wisdom or Buddhist wisdom or Christian wisdom. It grows without being named, without the need for a name, even the name "wisdom". Wisdom may appear to be foolishness to others, but it is not. It shows orderliness and purposefulness and ultimate harmlessness and meaningfulness.

In moments of wisdom we aren't concerned with whether we are wise or foolish, we aren't troubled by what others think of our decisions, we continue our course because it is the right course. Yet we take into consideration other perspectives and possibilities. Such wisdom is a gift of great value. Treasure those moments. You increase the likelihood of such moments with a disciplined life of purpose. A feeling-dominated life is nearsighted and unsuited to moments of wisdom.

7

You need both moments of quiet and moments of activity. All moments find increased value in focus, attentiveness, purpose, and diligence. Be aware of settings and circumstances, your physical and mental state, the beckoning of the situation. Respond with alertness to the response to your response. Adapt yourself to the changing situation. Rebound from occasional carelessness with care. Who do you think you are to reproach yourself? Just get back to living well.

Sleepiness is affected by physical movement and by sleeping. You get no extra credit for staying awake unnecessarily, and your health may suffer. However, when you are awake, behave so that you are fully awake. Moments of drowsy dullness waste precious opportunities. Get moving. Lose yourself in something.

This moment requests your immediate attention. It is all you have to work with in order to construct your life. Tomorrow is a concept within which you can do nothing. Do not forget that resting is action, too. Only you can decide what needs doing now.

REFLECTIONS ON HAN SHAN

After reading Chan Master Han Shan 1546-1623 (Text Translated by Upasaka Richard Cheung and paraphrased by Rev. Chuan Yuan (Ming Zhen) Shakya, OHY) I find points of agreement and disagreement as well as points that seem unrealistic or vague allowing me to substitute unrelated material. You might wish to compare the original found on the Internet with these CL reflections.

1. Some people will never embrace Constructive Living. They are content with their unrealistic fantasies. They have invested themselves in studies and degrees and communities hoping for some sort of wish fulfillment. Our job is not to convince or convert; it is to make available a realistic alternative.

2. Ignore the material world at your peril. Drown in the material world at your peril. Learn to see both surface and below the surface.

3. Desires result in both joy and sorrow. Desires are natural phenomena to be accepted as they are. Desires are neither our masters nor our slaves.

4. I have books on the shelf I won't live long enough to read. I have clothes that will not wear out before I die. I don't need the very latest electronic devices. What would you trade for the guarantee of an extra year of healthy life? Material objects are not unimportant. Know the relative value of what you call yours.

5. Whatever you own disappears from your mind when you lose yourself in some task. However the task turns out you disappear within it. Something lost, something found. Appreciate your treasure.

6. No one sees all events with equanimity. No one avoids pain and disappointment. What is possible is to view pain and disappointment and joy and love and other feelings from another perspective. Instead of brandishing the weapons of oughts and ought nots, we can cruise along on the vehicle of what is.

7. What tactics and strategies have worked well for us in the past? What tactics and strategies are suggested in these lines? Trial and error show us what is worthy of our time and effort. Reality is the best teacher, responding to what we do and not to what we think or intend.

8. Don't trust Constructive Living or David Reynolds or anything else except your experience. We offer hints for living that work well for us, but you can validate or reject those hints for yourself. Most often you know what you need to do; the trouble may be doing what you know needs doing. You fix that problem on your own.

9. What appear to be small actions can have large consequences. So carry out even everyday routine tasks with attention and care. Build your life on actions of detailed appreciation and finesse. To do otherwise would be a waste of your potential and an opening for unnecessary misery.

10. Choose your goals wisely. It is so difficult to do two things well at the same time. Fix the spotlight of your attention on worthy goals, but allow enough leeway to keep up with your surroundings. Changes in your environment affect the accomplishment of your goals.

11. It is proper to offer a morning greeting whether you receive a response or not. Why do you think of it as a risk to do so? Why do you feel exposed when no response is forthcoming? How fortunate we are to be able to greet others.

12. Wealth opens some doors and closes others. Drawers and closets become overfull. Locks are added to deter loss by theft. Time is invested in safeguarding and building more wealth. Expectations of others go up as resources increase. Keeping up appearances requires more attention. One mistake can prove financially costly. Yes, profits involve costs, too.

13. You will be sometimes happy, sometimes sad, sometimes full of hope, sometimes despairing, sometimes refreshed, sometimes exhausted. Life is like that for everyone. A life of peaceful calmness would be boring; no one is bored that way.

14. Thoughts fly into your mind from nowhere. You have some gatekeeping control, but it is not absolute. Rather than strictly standing guard at the gate, you would do well to read and speak and watch and listen to what is realistic and good. Open the gate widely to allow in a flood of desirable thoughts.

15. Everyone is sometimes stupid, sometimes overlooking what needs to be done, sometimes overly careful. What is important is what you do next after discovering your error. Trying to conceal your mistake is usually not the most important thing to do next.

16. Food preferences, values, perceptions of beauty, and skills vary from person to person. I have no right to dictate your behavior, but I can make suggestions and educate about consequences for actions. You decide what you need to do. You must live with consequences.

17. I have grown old thanks to genes and food and shelter and medical care and meaningful activities and safety practices all provided by other people. I could have died in a car accident or in a medical prescription error or on a mountain trail mishap or a plane crash. How can I repay those who made this life now possible?

18. Advice about living well comes from many sources. The major faith that is necessary is faith in your own judgment about what is true and realistic. Your life experience will inform you about

the merits and faults in various lifeways. As you accumulate wisdom about how to live well, you have responsibility to actually do so.

19. Well-placed effort is valuable no matter what the results of that effort. There is no guarantee that anyone will read these words. Nevertheless, I am obliged to write them. I can offer stories about why I have this obligation, but you should know by now to be skeptical of such stories. Stories or not I am obligated to make this effort.

20. You and I are going to die. There is no doubt about it. Doing life well includes dying well. Preparing for death is part of living well. Dying well means doing all that can be done until nothing more can be done. Dying well does not necessarily involve peaceful feelings or joy. Dying offers just another occasion for doing life well.

21. There are both penalties and rewards associated with public honor and fame. The temptation to use public status to achieve unseemly goals is strong. The fear of falling from grace may be equally strong. The goal of using one's status to be useful to others helps to keep actions on a constructive track.

22. The objective amount of money one possesses is not a good measure of one's satisfaction with personal finances. For some, the amount of money possessed is never enough. For others, a small amount is sufficient. Satisfaction and dissatisfaction are tied to purposes, not possessions.

23. It is a fiction that brains and talent and righteousness will necessarily bring rewards in this world. When your priorities are properly aligned the rewards of this world are minor factors.

Honor and esteem and recognition are trivial compared to purposefully and constructively using life well. It is preferable to be useful to others and unknown than to be popular and respected.

24. Don't think that you can escape death. Don't expect your memory and deeds and institutions and corporations to live on for centuries after you die. What matters is how you are living today. What you do today is that which is most under your control. The sharpest judge of what you do today is yourself.

25. You can't know everything about anything. Everything keeps changing, including you. Even words that look alike and sound alike vary from moment to moment. These words, too. Nevertheless, let us slip and stumble along while wading through running water. It is impossible to stand still anyway. Immobility is not an option.

26. Praise and rewards are more effective in the long run than complaints and punishment when trying to influence another's behavior. Understandable explanations about why an action is preferable are more effective in the long run than dictating rules from a position of power. Note the first word in that last sentence.

27. Although I sometimes set an alarm clock to be safe, I haven't used an alarm to wake up in years. The secret is to go to sleep early. No special magical powers are necessary. Life presents many opportunities to avoid potential problems by behaving sensibly in advance.

28. We use the word "dirty" to refer to shoes and minds and habits. Though the word is the same, the meanings differ. Similarly we use the word "my" to refer to a house, a mind, a family, a thought, an emotion, health and so forth--each with unique meaning. Beware thinking that the

consistency of a word implies consistency in that for which it stands. My sorrow yesterday is not my sorrow today, and neither are mine in the sense of owning them.

29. Too much worrying is a problem. Too little worrying is also a problem. "Don't worry" we say as though worries could be turned on and off at will. Returning focus to controllable behaviors and reasonable goals keeps worries within bounds. Think of worrying as a hobby, not a symptom.

30. A problem is merely a question about what needs doing next. Sometimes the answer is to turn away from the problem and do something else that is more urgent. Sometimes the answer is to attack the problem even though one's actions are unlikely to resolve the matter. Knowing what needs to be done may be easier than actually doing it.

31. We all live on borrowed time with borrowed bodies. Our thoughts and feelings, too, are borrowed. As recipients of such largesse, we are obliged to use these treasures well. Whether we feel grateful or not, our debts must be repaid with actions.

32. Even the best of us has moments of greed and anger and arrogance. What behaviors encourage such qualities? What needs doing when those moments of shallowness appear?

33. Over years of living one gets to know the habits of one's mind. Such understanding allows for anticipation of upcoming moments. The anticipation allows for desired change. Awareness of mental trends brings both increased flexibility and increased responsibility.

34. Sensitivity to the faults in others is often stimulated by the same faults in oneself. Check out your own tendencies when the urge to criticise another emerges.

35. For the most part laws are made by and for those with power. Whatever the laws, you are obligated to do what is right. Consider the effects of your behavior on others--living others and other others.

36. It isn't necessary to convince others that Constructive Living is a sensible way to live. Fortunately, reality takes care of that. People use what is useful.

37. Wealth opens certain options and closes others. So do aging, education, marriage, children, religion, business promotions, and CL. Be alert to changes in possibilities as circumstances change.

38. Alertness to change can be obscured by all sorts of things. Emotions, over-focus on one goal, success, failure, poor health, and lack of sleep are examples of factors that can influence our ability to notice changes in our life situations.

39. Where does the answer to a math problem come from as it enters my mind? When a challenge appears what causes me to think of behavioral solutions? What puts these words into my thoughts so I can input them into this computer? Wrong or right, the life responses that come to mind are gifts from an unknown source.

40. Life takes unexpected turns. What at first appears to be an easy course may turn out to be quite difficult. What appears at first to be a difficult course may turn out to go smoothly with little effort. However the course turns out we should act on the best course in this moment. Remember that doing nothing is also a course--one that may be the best or the worst course.

41. No one controls his or her emotions. They cannot be controlled and need not be controlled. Whatever emotions emerge naturally and spontaneously we are responsible for what we do. Even when emotions cloud our perception and judgment, we are responsible for what we do. No excuses.

42. It is easier to discern the faults of others than one's own faults. It is easier to criticise others than to criticise oneself. Criticise your criticism of others to find their good points and discover your own sensitivity to those areas of criticism. You may discover your own personal versions of the faults you find in others. When others criticise or scold me, I am most likely to become angry when the criticism is at least partially justified; I am at least partly to blame.

43. Success may lead you to be less tolerant of others. Comparing your own success with the mediocrity of others may lead to arrogance, insensitivity, and contempt. Remember to appreciate and thank those who made your success possible.

44. We cannot, need not, should not eliminate desires. The push and pull of desires give us information about what needs to be done. Desires do not provide all the information about what needs to be done. Other information is needed, as well. Acting only on the prompting of desires will lead to trouble. So invite desires as guests into your home, but invite other guests, too. Experience, education, ethics, customs, laws, and other humans are welcome guests, too, with information worthy of your attention.

45. We are all deeply embedded in life. The shifting flows of events and habits of thought and behavior drag us here and there. Noticing the forces that affect us and how we are affected is a first

step in finding some measure of freedom within the currents. Pay attention even when in the midst of some automatic routine. Find moments of freedom to refine your life.

46. Actions have consequences. The size of the actions don't always match the consequences. Consequences are often unnoticed, unanticipated, and undeserved. If you think that conscious thought causes actions you are grossly oversimplifying. Watch the hands and feet of anyone who is engaged in a conversation. Notice how your feet may lead you to a place, and then you discover why you went there.

47. People who feel sorry for themselves have too much time on their hands and not enough purpose. They also lack focus on what is provided to them moment by moment. If their health permits, at a minimum they need to get moving. Taking a walk is a start.

48. Sometimes we fail. Sometimes others notice our failure. Sometimes the failure has major consequences, sometimes not. In any case, what needs doing next?

49. Change happens. It causes us to discover and to let go, to win and to lose. The pace of change changes, too. We can't preserve the now, no matter how desirable it appears. There is no choice but to go with the flow.

50. I recommend going to bed early, a couple of hours after your last meal. Such a custom allows early rising for a rested start on your day. Getting into bed is controllable; getting to sleep is not. It may take some time until your body adjusts to the rhythm of early to bed and early to rise.

51. One way children and adults learn is by imitation. Be a model of constructive behavior. Respect is earned through your behavior; it is the only aspect of your life that others can see.

52. You cannot know directly what others think and feel. You can make educated guesses about how your behavior will affect others. You can imagine what others are thinking and feeling as a result of your behavior. Walk carefully in life.

53. There is something beyond what you think and feel; it is not just your brain. I cannot show it to you because it is beyond what anyone can show and outside of what anyone can see. So looking for it is just a waste of time. Momentarily dissolving into it is possible.

54. When the tennis stroke or golf swing plays itself, when the flower draws itself, when the car drives itself, when the broom sweeps itself, then there is a special satisfaction. Even when the right words appear during a speech or during a session of writing, there is satisfaction. Sometimes I get out of the way and let Reality happen.

55. When I stop to notice these events, this satisfaction, then they are gone. My ego is unable to turn them back on at will. Reality happens.

56. No one can undo a murder. To think we can rehabilitate a murderer is prideful foolishness. Events of the past are frozen; many cannot be superficially thawed by the heat of present actions.

57. Our bodies are borrowed. They will eventually be returned. Use them wisely, aiming to repay the debt.

58. Imagining what came before birth or what comes after death is just imagining. No one knows. We know what came before others were born and what came after others died, but such knowledge is of no use in solving the puzzles of our own birth and death. To call them puzzles is once more a product of our imagination. Our minds are built to classify and sort and wonder why and how.

59. I do not know your genuine purposes and motives. I don't know why I do what I do, though I can tell you many stories about why. Talk about motives and purposes is socially constructed to satisfy our minds, not to discover the elusive truth. All motives are hidden, no matter what we believe or tell others.

60. All knowledge is socially constructed to satisfy ourselves and others. Even scientists aim for acceptance of their theories and findings by their peers. To achieve acknowledgment of our knowledge we must communicate successfully. Such is my aim here. Or so I write. The fact of my writing cannot be denied while pondering my aims.

61. Keep your life purposeful. Your long-term goals, however distant, should have more immediate purposeful steps. Keeping your attention on immediate purposes, however small, keeps life focused and meaningful. Allow natural distractions to suggest new purposes. Ask yourself again and again, "What is my purpose now?"

62. You cannot quash a feeling by force of will. You cannot make desires go away. When you realize, again and again, how to recognize and accept and learn from feelings and desires without being governed by them, then you are on the road to a constructive life.

63. Going through daily life reflexively, automatically, is boring. Paying attention to changes in your environment and responding to them with awareness of purpose is much more interesting and is likely to be more fruitful. Develop the habit of periodically scanning your environment and your behavior to discover new possibilities.

64. Life comes with many details. The details are important, too, but you must learn which details require your response and which details can be left alone. Perfectionism is unrealistic; so is slothful inattention to detail. Pay attention to outcomes and develop the skill of parsing your perspective.

65. While your mind is soaring through the clouds don't stumble on the stairs.

66. The wise teachers of old wore clothes, ate food, sought shelter in storms. Someone used tools to record their teachings. Their material possessions were borrowed then, as ours are borrowed now. Nothing is mine alone.

67. Why work? To repay the world for your existence and support, to keep on learning and developing, for the income that increases your possibilities and reduces your debt.

68. No one has everything he or she wants. Wants always outpace accomplishments.

69. No one consistently avoids comparisons between self and other. Emphasizing our similarities helps to reduce judgments both positive and negative. Nevertheless, I am more like me than anyone else, and I was born with a lifetime guarantee.

70. Self-focus is both the cause and result of suffering. Moments beyond self-focus are more interesting and more instructive and more misery-free.

71. The people you enjoy being around are people who consider the convenience of others. Self-centered people are irksome. Self-centeredness becomes increasingly unacceptable as one ages.

72. Rebels provide alternative perspectives. Watch for whose convenience the rebel is rebelling. Some perspectives are worth more than others. Rebellion per se is not necessarily valuable.

73. Humor and laughter help us to lose ourselves. Sorrow and grief turn our attention to ourselves. Something causes us to seek freedom from ourselves and to avoid immersing ourselves in self-focus.

74. Change keeps happening. Change keeps life interesting and unstable. Words conceal the changes that occur by appearing to be the same each time they are encountered.

75. There are two ways to recognize truth of any sort--suddenly or gradually. Insight may hit your instantly or experience may build up to a conclusion. However you come by it, truth is always truth.

76. Truths described by words are nested within larger truths described by words. The most encompassing truths aren't described by words at all. It is improper to call them "truths" at all.

77. Why do you suppose I keep using words to warn you about words? Your senses offer the same warnings. Your memories may not.

78. The mind chatters away even when lips are closed. Reduce the chatter with focused attention. Don't miss the wordless message.

REFLECTIONS ON NIETZCHE'S BEYOND GOOD AND EVIL

I'm using here the translation by Helen Zimmern of Friedrich Nietzche's fourth chapter, APOPHTHEGMS AND INTERLUDES. Nietzche's numbering system continues through the chapters; so the fourth chapter begins with item number 63

63. He who is a thorough teacher takes things seriously--and even himself--only in relation to his pupils. Constructive Living--Why even to them?

64. "Knowledge for its own sake" Constructive Living--I don't understand this phrase. Knowledge may turn out to be useful in unexpected ways.

65. The charm of knowledge would be small, were it not so much shame has to be overcome on the way to it. Constructive Living--What shame?

65A. We are most dishonourable towards our God: he is not PERMITTED to sin. Constructive Living--Reality is as it is.

66. The tendency of a person to allow himself to be degraded, robbed, deceived, and exploited might be the diffidence of a God among men. Constructive Living--Established religious people are responsible for their actions, too.

67. Love to one only is a barbarity, for it is exercised at the expense of all others. Love to God also! The notion that love is a limited resource that is purposely directed is false. Constructive Living-- Agreed. Love happens to us, it has no limits.

68. "I did that," says my memory. "I could not have done that," says my pride, and remains inexorable. Eventually--the memory yields. Constructive Living--Not mine.

69. One has regarded life carelessly, if one has failed to see the hand that--kills with leniency. Constructive Living--Killing is killing.

70. If a man has character, he has also his typical experience, which always recurs. Constructive Living--Habits are likely to produce similar experiences (not the same experiences and not all the time).

71. THE SAGE AS ASTRONOMER. So long as thou feelest the stars as an "above thee," thou lackest the eye of the discerning one. Constructive Living--Keep an eye on what is real.

72. It is not the strength, but the duration of great sentiments that makes great men. Constructive Living--Any sentiments come and go to all men.

73. He who attains his ideal, precisely thereby surpasses it. Constructive Living--We change moment by moment, sometimes attaining, sometimes not. Ideals are never attained once and for all.

73A. Many a peacock hides his tail from every eye--and calls it his pride. Constructive Living-- Those with time to hide or show off their accomplishments are distracted from more accomplishments.

74. A man of genius is unbearable, unless he possess at least two things besides: gratitude and purity. Constructive Living--Both gratitude and purity come and go.

75. The degree and nature of a man's sensuality extends to the highest altitudes of his spirit. Constructive Living--Just talk. What do these clever words mean?

76. Under peaceful conditions the militant man attacks himself. Constructive Living--Sometimes; sometimes he searches for more victims.

77. With his principles a man seeks either to dominate, or justify, or honour, or reproach, or conceal his habits: two men with the same principles probably seek fundamentally different ends therewith. Constructive Living--Purposes and intentions in others are difficult to ascertain.

78. He who despises himself, nevertheless esteems himself thereby, as a despiser. Constructive Living--Yes, doubt your doubts; then doubt your ability to doubt your doubts, and so forth.

79. A soul which knows that it is loved, but does not itself love, betrays its sediment: its dregs come up. Constructive Living--Love is a feeling, uncontrollable like all feelings. Love happens to us and is not directed by will (whatever that might be).

80. A thing that is explained ceases to concern us. Constructive Living--Tell that to a pedestrian crossing a foggy street and seeing an approaching car.

81. It is terrible to die of thirst at sea. Is it necessary that you should so salt your truth that it will no longer quench thirst? Constructive Living--Truth is truth, tasteless or not.

82. "Sympathy for all" would be harshness and tyranny for THEE, my good neighbour. Constructive Living--An imagined possibility, but unrealistic.

83. INSTINCT--When the house is on fire one forgets even the dinner. Constructive Living--Yes, but one recovers appetite later from among the ashes.

84. Woman learns how to hate in proportion as she forgets how to charm. Constructive Living--No one has to learn how to hate. Hate happens.

85. The same emotions are in man and woman, but in different TEMPO, on that account man and woman never cease to misunderstand each other. Constructive Living--Misunderstanding happens because of emotional and cognitive differences among the sexes, probably with evolutionary roots.

86. In the background of all their personal vanity, women themselves have still their impersonal scorn for "woman". Constructive Living--Scorn is invariably personal.

87. FETTERED HEART, FREE SPIRIT--When one firmly fetters one's heart and keeps it prisoner, one can allow one's spirit many liberties: I said this once before but people do not believe it when I say so, unless they know it already. Constructive Living--Show me a fettered heart and the way to control it; then I'll believe it.

88. One begins to distrust very clever persons when they become embarrassed. Constructive Living--Surprise and embarrassment may indeed reveal aspects of someone who carries a facade of cleverness.

89. Dreadful experiences raise the question whether he who experiences them is not something dreadful also. Constructive Living--We are all sometimes dreadful, sometimes not.

90. Heavy, melancholy men turn lighter, and come temporarily to their surface, precisely by that which makes others heavy: by hatred and love. Constructive Living--Just talk. No one has a simple explanation of why people change.

91. So cold, so icy, that one burns one's finger at the touch of him! Every hand that lays hold of him shrinks back! And for that very reason many think him red-hot. Constructive Living--Show me the data behind this string of words.

92. Who has not, at one time or another sacrificed himself for the sake of his good name? Constructive Living--"Himself" is vague. Specify what was lost and what was gained and what is meant by "sacrifice."

93. In affability there is no hatred of men, but precisely on that account a great deal too much contempt of men. Constructive Living--Affability is as affability does. Who knows the motives?

94. The maturity of man that means, to have reacquired the seriousness that one had as a child at play. Constructive Living--Seriousness in children, too, comes and goes during play.

95. To be ashamed of one's immorality is a step on the ladder at the end of which one is ashamed also of one's morality. Constructive Living--Buy into an ideal moral standard and one is assured of failure.

96. One should part from life as Ulysses parted from Nausicaa: blessing it rather than in love with it. Constructive Living--Blessing is behavior; love is uncontrollable.

97. What? A great man? I always see merely the play-actor of his own ideal. Constructive Living--Greatness is always in the eye of the beholder.

98. When one trains one's conscience, it kisses one while it bites. Constructive Living--Comparisons bring both success and failure.

99. THE DISAPPOINTED ONE SPEAKS:I listened for the echo and I heard only praise. Constructive Living--High standards yield both disappointment and satisfaction.

100. We all feign to ourselves that we are simpler than we are, we thus relax ourselves away from our fellows. Constructive Living--We are all sometimes this, sometimes that.

101. A discerning one might easily regard himself at present as the animalization of God. Constructive Living--Pinch yourself, then define "God".

102. Discovering reciprocal love should really disenchant the lover with regard to the beloved. "What! She is modest enough to love even you? Or stupid enough? Or--or---" Constructive Living--Feelings happen; interpretations are add-ons.

103. THE DANGER IN HAPPINESS. --"Everything now turns out best for me, I now love every fate:--who would like to be my fate?" Constructive Living--Fate is not an explanation; it is word play.

104. Not their love of humanity, but the impotence of their love, prevents the Christians of today--burning us. Constructive Living--All attempts to explain why behavior occurs is subject to doubt.

105. The pia fraus is still more repugnant to the taste (the "piety") of the free spirit (the "pious man of knowledge") than the impia fraus. Hence the profound lack of judgment, in comparison with the

Church, characteristic of the type "free spirit"--as ITS non-freedom. Constructive Living—It is Nietzche's playfulness with obscure strings of words that is here apparent.

106. By means of music the very passions enjoy themselves. Constructive Living--Feelings are not creatures.

107. A sign of strong character, when once the resolution has been taken, to shut the ear even to the best counter-arguments. Occasionally, therefore, a will to stupidity. Constructive Living--Keep inputting relevant information, even while acting on earlier information.

108. There is no such thing as moral phenomena, but only a moral interpretation of phenomena. Constructive Living--Here we agree, interpreting Nietzche's interpretation.

109. The criminal is often enough not equal to his deed: he extenuates and maligns it. Constructive Living--Many criminals do seem to be neither thoughtful nor skillful at doing what they do.

110. The advocates of a criminal are seldom artists enough to turn the beautiful terribleness of the deed to the advantage of the doer. Constructive Living--What is beautiful about something terrible?

111. Our vanity is most difficult to wound just when our pride has been wounded. Constructive Living--The subtle distinction between vanity and pride here escapes me.

112. To him who feels himself preordained to contemplation and not to belief, all believers are too noisy and obtrusive; he guards against them. Constructive Living--All contemplation implies beliefs of some sort.

113. "You want to prepossess him in your favour? Then you must be embarrassed before him." Constructive Living--Such a tactic may work well, or it may result in disdain.

114. The immense expectation with regard to sexual love, and the coyness in this expectation, spoils all the perspectives of women at the outset. Constructive Living—Here, again, he pontificates too broadly. Are all women like this all the time?

115. Where there is neither love nor hatred in the game, woman's play is mediocre. Constructive Living--Too narrow a perspective of women's behavior.

116. The great epochs of our life are at the points when we gain courage to rebaptize our badness as the best in us. Constructive Living--For example? Courage or not we can reinterpret life elements.

117. The will to overcome an emotion, is ultimately only the will of another, or of several other, emotions. Constructive Living--Will is a meaningless term inferred from behavior. Emotions need not and cannot be overcome.

118. There is an innocence of admiration: it is possessed by him to whom it has not yet occurred that he himself may be admired some day. Constructive Living--How self-centered; deserved admiration is independent of status of the admirer. Admiration, like any feeling, happens.

119. Our loathing of dirt may be so great as to prevent our cleaning ourselves;"justifying" ourselves. Constructive Living—Here is another excuse for failing to do what needs doing.

120. Sensuality often forces the growth of love too much, so that its root remains weak, and is easily torn up. Constructive Living--And ego's self-convenience is the tool that tears it.

121. It is a curious thing that God learned Greek when he wished to turn author--and that he did not learn it better. Constructive Living--Human learning and human perspective are limited.

122. To rejoice on account of praise is in many cases merely politeness of heart--and the very opposite of vanity of spirit. Constructive Living--When praised express thanks whatever one feels.

123. Even concubinage has been corrupted--by marriage. --And power by authority, thievery by banks, etc. Constructive Living--Human attempts to socialize and structure forms of behavior have a long history.

124. He who exults at the stake, does not triumph over pain, but because of the fact that he does not feel pain where he expected it. A parable. Constructive Living--Parables of pain are easier to construct when the author is not in pain.

125. When we have to change an opinion about any one, we charge heavily to his account the inconvenience he thereby causes us. Constructive Living--And we ignore the inconvenience we have caused him.

126. A nation is a detour of nature to arrive at six or seven great men. Constructive Living— Perhaps, and then to get around them. We all die.

127. In the eyes of all true women science is hostile to the sense of shame. They feel as if one wished to peep under their skin with it—or worse still! under their dress and finery. Constructive Living--My mother said that a woman never exposes everything, but I suspect that a man is no different. Exceptions and momentary change make broad generalizations of this sort tenuous.

128. The more abstract the truth you wish to teach, the more must you allure the senses to it. Constructive Living--Tack down concepts to concrete reality or risk playing with froth, as here.

129. The devil has the most extensive perspectives for God; on that account he keeps so far away from him: the devil, in effect, as the oldest friend of knowledge. Constructive Living--Constructive Living perspectives on feelings offer distance, too, but the perspectives don't eliminate feelings.

130. What a person IS begins to betray itself when his talent decreases, when he ceases to show what he CAN do. Talent is also an adornment; an adornment is also a concealment. Constructive Living--What a person IS changes moment by moment. Adornments conceal because we cannot perceive all things at once; attention has limits.

131. The sexes deceive themselves about each other: the reason is that in reality they honour and love only themselves (or their own ideal, to express it more agreeably). Thus man wishes woman to be peaceable: but in fact woman is ESSENTIALLY unpeaceable, like the cat, however well she may have assumed the peaceable demeanour. Constructive Living—More of Nietzche's static sexist nonsense.

132. One is punished best for one's virtues. Constructive Living--Virtues and punishment and rewards are momentary and sometimes temporally unrelated.

133. He who cannot find the way to HIS ideal, lives more frivolously and shamelessly than the man without an ideal. Constructive Living--Who is without purposes, goals, ideals?

134. From the senses originate all trustworthiness, all good conscience, all evidence of truth. Constructive Living--Sensory information is interpreted, made into meaning of all sorts.

135. Pharisaism is not a deterioration of the good man; a considerable part of it is rather an essential condition of being good. Constructive Living--Sometimes this, sometimes that, sometimes back and forth.

136. The one seeks an accoucheur for his thoughts, the other seeks some one whom he can assist: a good conversation thus originates. Constructive Living--How kind of others to listen to us and respond!

137. In intercourse with scholars and artists one readily makes mistakes of opposite kinds: in a remarkable scholar one not infrequently finds a mediocre man; and often, even in a mediocre artist, one finds a very remarkable man. Constructive Living--There is no guarantee that skill or mediocrity in one area insures skill or mediocrity in another. As in many of Nietzche's casual generalizations we lack data from a large sample.

138. We do the same when awake as when dreaming: we only invent and imagine him with whom we have intercourse--and forget it immediately. Constructive Living--Minds move from topic to topic. "So long," Nietzche; "So long," Constructive Living.

139. In revenge and in love woman is more barbarous than man. Constructive Living--One wonders what experiences prompted this statement and how "barbarous" is defined.

140. ADVICE AS A RIDDLE. --"If the band is not to break, bite it first--secure to make!" Constructive Living--No amount of effort assures a desired result, but the odds can be improved by appropriate action.

141. The belly is the reason why man does not so readily take himself for a God. Constructive Living--Beware any explanation for thought or behavior, including a non-explanation such as this one. "Beware" does not mean "avoid", only retain some doubt. Explanations can be useful, if kept in place.

142. The chastest utterance I ever heard: "Dans le veritable amour c'est l'ame qui enveloppe le corps." Constructive Living--All feelings (including true love) have physical and mental aspects.

143. Our vanity would like what we do best to pass precisely for what is most difficult to us. Constructive Living--Nietzche's generalization may apply to some systems of morals, as well. However, exceptions abound.

144. When a woman has scholarly inclinations there is generally something wrong with her sexual nature. Barrenness itself conduces to a certain virility of taste; man, indeed, if I may say so, is "the barren animal." Constructive Living—Whether this sexist thinking was true or not in his day, it is certainly not so today.

145. Comparing man and woman generally, one may say that woman would not have the genius for adornment, if she had not the instinct for the SECONDARY role. Constructive Living—Both sexes have interest in adornment these days; beware simple explanations, even those based on fMRI data. Again, whether Nietzche's sexist thinking was true or not in his day, it is certainly not so today.

146. He who fights with monsters should be careful lest he thereby become a monster. And if thou gaze long into an abyss, the abyss will also gaze into thee. Constructive Living—Focused attention does have an affect on the brain and on future behavior (for better or for worse).

147. From old Florentine novels--moreover, from life: Buona femmina e mala femmina vuol bastone. Constructive Living—There are no good or bad men or women, only good or bad moments evaluated momentarily.

148. To seduce their neighbour to a favourable opinion, and afterwards to believe implicitly in this opinion of their neighbour--who can do this conjuring trick so well as women? Constructive Living—It is not unusual to believe what one wants to believe, whatever the gender.

149. That which an age considers evil is usually an unseasonable echo of what was formerly considered good--the atavism of an old ideal. Constructive Living—Even Nietzche's attempt to modify his broad generalization with"usually" seems excessive here. Beware extreme pronouncements.

150. Around the hero everything becomes a tragedy; around the demigod everything becomes a satyr-play; and around God everything becomes--what? perhaps a "world"? Constructive Living—Around Nietzsche's world are too many words.

151. It is not enough to possess a talent: one must also have your permission to possess it—eh, my friends? Constructive Living—talents are socially defined.

152. "Where there is the tree of knowledge, there is always Paradise": so say the most ancient and the most modern serpents. Constructive Living—The knowledge tree drops its leaves and a variety of plants emerge from the ground.

153. What is done out of love always takes place beyond good and evil. Constructive Living—There are varieties of love—some laudable, some self-focused.

154. Objection, evasion, joyous distrust, and love of irony are signs of health; everything absolute belongs to pathology. Constructive Living—Absolute talk may be a sign of neuroticism or laziness. So may be objection, evasion, joyous distrust, and love of irony. Anything that pulls one from reality is suspect.

155. The sense of the tragic increases and declines with sensuousness. Constructive Living—The sense of the tragic increases and declines with unoccupied time and boredom.

156. Insanity in individuals is something rare--but in groups, parties, nations, and epochs it is the rule. Constructive Living—Nietzsche's diagnostic criteria are undisclosed, so his generalities are questionable.

157. The thought of suicide is a great consolation: by means of it one gets successfully through many a bad night. Constructive Living—One would hope for more constructive methods of getting through a bad night.

158. Not only our reason, but also our conscience, truckles to our strongest impulse--the tyrant in us. Constructive Living—Sometimes tyrant, sometimes gentle respondent.

159. One MUST repay good and ill; but why just to the person who did us good or ill? Constructive Living—Reciprocity is found in all human cultures, but the "MUST" is found in Nietzsche.

160. One no longer loves one's knowledge sufficiently after one has communicated it. Constructive Living—Knowledge is not mine to love like a possession. I am no more than a method for communicating certain kinds of knowledge.

161. Poets act shamelessly towards their experiences: they exploit them. Constructive Living—We all use our borrowed experiences to communicate with borrowed tools.

162. "Our fellow-creature is not our neighbour, but our neighbour's neighbour":--so thinks every nation. Constructive Living—Show me a nation. Show me a nation that thinks. You only see this person and that person and so forth. I can see my neighbors. Don't get lost in abstract words.

163. Love brings to light the noble and hidden qualities of a lover—his rare and exceptional traits: it is thus liable to be deceptive as to his normal character. Constructive Living—Behavior may change with love. But "character" and "normal" are wisps of verbal fantasy.

164. Jesus said to his Jews: "The law was for servants;--love God as I love him, as his Son! What have we Sons of God to do with morals!" Constructive Living—You decide what you need to do. Be prepared to take the consequences from society and from conscience.

165. IN SIGHT OF EVERY PARTY. A shepherd has always need of a bell-wether--or he has himself to be a wether occasionally. Constructive Living—Thanks to followers there are leaders.

166. One may indeed lie with the mouth; but with the accompanying grimace one nevertheless tells the truth. Constructive Living—Some are more skillful at lying than others. Some are more skillful at perceiving lies than others.

167. To vigorous men intimacy is a matter of shame--and something precious. Constructive Living—Intimacy is a rare gift, deserving thanks.

168. Christianity gave Eros poison to drink; he did not die of it, certainly, but degenerated to Vice. Constructive Living—Erotic feelings are not uncommon; erotic behavior has various cultural and historical definitions.

169. To talk much about oneself may also be a means of concealing oneself. Constructive Living—Concealing oneself from oneself and from others takes various forms. Talk of any sort runs the risk of concealing what is.

170. In praise there is more obtrusiveness than in blame. Constructive Living—Maximize praise; minimize blame. Behavioral research shows such a tactic is most effective in influencing others.

171. Pity has an almost ludicrous effect on a man of knowledge, like tender hands on a Cyclops. Constructive Living—We are all pitifully ignorant of the details of the magnitude of our gifts from Reality.

172. One occasionally embraces some one or other, out of love to mankind (because one cannot embrace all); but this is what one must never confess to the individual. Constructive Living—We want to be embraced as individuals, not as representatives, but the one who embraces others as individuals rather than representatives benefits more.

173. One does not hate as long as one disesteems, but only when one esteems equal or superior. Constructive Living—Beware any explanations of the causes of emotions. My wife hates worms.

174. Ye Utilitarians--ye, too, love the UTILE only as a VEHICLE for your inclinations,--ye, too, really find the noise of its wheels insupportable! Constructive Living—We do tend to prefer philosophies that validate our preferences. We tend to ignore and discount other philosophies and theories that do not fit with our preferences. Constructive Living is no exception.

175. One loves ultimately one's desires, not the thing desired. Constructive Living—Desires come, and desires go. Use the information from desires to assist in determining what needs to be done.

176. The vanity of others is only counter to our taste when it is counter to our vanity. Constructive Living—What makes my taste so important? Vanity is based on a misunderstanding of where we fit in Reality.

177. With regard to what "truthfulness" is, perhaps nobody has ever been sufficiently truthful. Constructive Living—We cannot notice everything at once. To pay attention to something is to ignore something else at that moment. "Reality is truth." (*Jijitsu yuishin*—Morita Masatake, M.D.)

178. One does not believe in the follies of clever men: what a forfeiture of the rights of man! Constructive Living—Clever humans make both clever and foolish mistakes. Who fails to believe it these days?

179. The consequences of our actions seize us by the forelock, very indifferent to the fact that we have meanwhile "reformed." Constructive Living—The past is fixed, unchangeable. However, our perspectives and memories of the past may result in reinterpretation.

180. There is an innocence in lying which is the sign of good faith in a cause. Constructive Living—Lying is most often self-serving, without innocence. The purpose is usually for one's own convenience.

181. It is inhuman to bless when one is being cursed. Constructive Living—It is difficult to bless when one is being cursed, but blessing is a controllable behavior. An attempt to take on the perspective of the person cursing may be helpful.

182. The familiarity of superiors embitters one, because it may not be returned. Constructive Living—It is also common these days for sellers to use the consumer's first name upon meeting him or her. Whether such a tactic is appreciated or scorned depends on the consumer.

183. "I am affected, not because you have deceived me, but because I can no longer believe in you." Constructive Living—There are many stories about possible cause here. Perhaps I am affected because I was foolish enough to believe in you at first. Perhaps I am affected because your deception reminds me of another deception. The point here is that simple explanation stories are suspect.

184. There is a haughtiness of kindness which has the appearance of wickedness. Constructive Living—Those who flaunt kindness are unkind. Showy humility is not humility. Showcased attention is narrowed attentiveness.

185. "I dislike him."--Why?--"I am not a match for him."--Did any one ever answer so? Constructive Living—Even honest attempts to explain feelings and behavior are misguided. Behavior can influence (but not control) subsequent feelings and behavior. What needs to be done next?

THE END

REFERENCES

Reynolds, David K.

Morita Psychotherapy, University of California Press, Berkeley, 1976.

The Quiet Therapies, University of Hawaii Press, Honolulu, 1980.

The Heart of the Japanese People, Nichieisha, Tokyo, 1980.

Naikan Psychotherapy, University of Chicago Press, 1983.

Constructive Living, University of Hawaii Press, Honolulu, 1984; Simon & Shuster, Australia.

Playing Ball on Running Water, Morrow, N.Y., 1984.

Living Lessons, Asahi, Tokyo, 1984.

Even in Summer the Ice Doesn't Melt. Morrow, N.Y., 1986.

Water Bears No Scars, Morrow, N.Y., 1987.

Constructive Living for Young People, Asahi, Tokyo, 1987.

Flowing Bridges, Quiet Waters, (ed.), SUNY Press, Albany, 1989.

Pools of Lodging for the Moon, Morrow, N.Y., 1989.

A Thousand Waves, Morrow, N.Y., 1990.

Thirsty, Swimming in the Lake, Morrow, N.Y., 1991.

Plunging Through the Clouds, (ed.) SUNY Press, Albany, 1993.

Rainbow Rising from a Stream, Morrow, N.Y., 1992.

Reflections on the Tao te Ching, Morrow, N.Y., 1993.

Light Waves: Fine Tuning the Mind. University of Hawaii Press, Honolulu, 2001.

A Handbook for Constructive Living, University of Hawaii Press, Honolulu, 2002.

See http://constructiveliving.org

See www.constructiveliving2.weebly.com